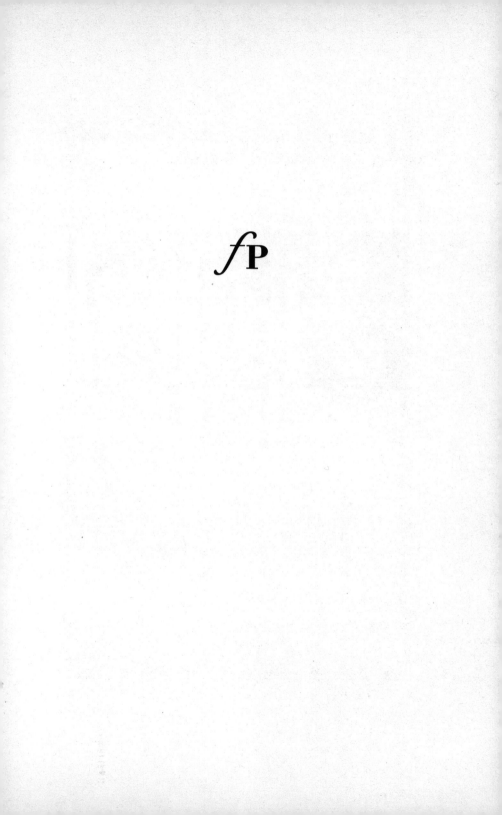

REWARD
Up to $10,000,000 USD
ABU MUSAB AL ZARQAWI

This man is wanted for murdering innocent women and children.

This terrorist born in Jordan also goes by the names:
Ahmed Al Kalaylah,
Fadel Nazzal Al Khalayleh,
Abu Mussab Al Zarqawi,
Abu Mussa Al Zarkawi

778-4076 Inside Bagdad
01-778-4076 Inside Iraq
964-01-778-4076 Outside Iraq
Email: tips@orha.centcom.mil

Your identity will remain secret

IZ C0825

HOW TO BREAK A TERRORIST

THE U.S. INTERROGATORS WHO USED
BRAINS, NOT BRUTALITY, TO TAKE DOWN
THE DEADLIEST MAN IN IRAQ

Matthew Alexander
with John R. Bruning

FREE PRESS

New York London Toronto Sydney

The views presented in this book are those of the author and do not reflect the official policy or position of the United States Air Force, the Department of Defense, or any other U.S. Government agency.

Free Press
A Division of Simon & Schuster, Inc.
1230 Avenue of the Americas
New York, NY 10020

First Free Press hardcover edition October 2008

Sources for photo insert:
Coalition Forces: Figs. 1, 3, 4, 5 6, 8
Hameed Rasheed/Associated Press: Fig. 2
Department of Defense: Figs. 7, 10
Karim Kadmin/Associated Press: Fig. 9
Matthew Alexander: Figs. 11, 12

For information about special discounts for bulk purchases, please contact Simon & Schuster Special Sales at 1-800-456-6798 or business@simonandschuster.com

Manufactured in the United States of America

1 3 5 7 9 10 8 6 4 2

Library of Congress Cataloging-in-Publication Data
Alexander, Matthew
How to Break a Terrorist : The U.S. interrogators who used brains, not brutality, to take down the deadliest man in Iraq / Matthew Alexander with John R. Bruning.
p. cm.
1. Terrorists. 2. Zarqawi, Abu Mus'ab, 1966–2006.
3. Qaida (Organization) 4. Alexander, Matthew.
5. Military interrogation. I. Bruning, John R. II. Title.
HV6433.M52A54 2008   956.7044'3—dc22
ISBN-13: 978-1-4165-7315-9
ISBN-10:   1-4165-7315-1

For the American soldiers and Iraqi civilians
who have died in this war.

Author's Note

IT WOULD BE impossible to recollect every word of every interrogation that I conducted or monitored in Iraq, but I've detailed these conversations as accurately as I could. I am writing under a pseudonym, and I have deliberately changed names and some operational details throughout to protect U.S. troops, ongoing missions, and the families of detainees from Al Qaida reprisals. This material was submitted to the Department of Defense for prepublication review and the blacked out material reflects deletions made by the DoD.

Contents

Contents

Foreword

by Mark Bowden

I GREW INTRIGUED BY the subject of interrogation in
2001, not long after the September 11 attacks, because
to combat small cells of terror-bent fanatics, the essen-
tial military tool would be not weaponry but knowledge.
How do you obtain information about a secretive enemy?
There would, of course, be spying, both electronic and
human. America is perhaps the most capable nation in the
world at the former and would have to get better fast at the
latter. The third tool, potentially the most useful and prob-
lematic, would be interrogation.

How do you get a captive to reveal critical, timely intelligence? I wrote about interrogation theory for *The Atlantic* in
2002 in an article called "The Dark Art of Interrogation,"
which predated the revelations of abuses at Abu Ghraib and
elsewhere. In the years since, the subject matter has become
predictably politically charged and highly controversial, with
liberals viewing harsher tactics as a sign of moral and legal
degeneration, and conservatives regarding attitudes toward
coercion as a litmus test of one's seriousness about the war
on "terror."

When I first met Matthew in 2007, it was a chance to learn exactly how our military was conducting high-level interrogations five years on. I was surprised (although I should not have been) to learn that a cadre of professional interrogators, or 'gators, had taken root inside the military: young men and women, some in uniform, others private contractors, who had years of hands-on experience interrogating prisoners in Afghanistan, Iraq, and elsewhere. It was heartening to learn from Matthew that the army had outgrown some of the earlier cruder methods of questioning. The quickest way to get most (but not all) captives talking is to be nice to them.

But what does it mean to be "nice" to a subject under interrogation? As Matthew's firsthand story of the intelligence operation that located and ultimately killed Abu Musab al Zarqawi illustrates, it often means one thing to the subject and another to the interrogator. It means, ideally, getting to know the subject better than he knows himself and then manipulating him by role-playing, flattering, misleading, and nudging his or her perception of the truth slightly off center. The goal is to turn the subject around so that he begins to see strong logic and even wisdom in acting against his own comrades and cause.

The greater part of the noise in media and politics over interrogation concerns the use of physical coercion, which is relevant to only a tiny fraction of the cases handled by military intelligence. The real work, as this book illustrates, can be far more challenging, complex, and interesting. The work could not be more important. Long after U.S. troops leave Iraq and even Afghanistan, the work of defeating Islamic fanatics will go on worldwide. We need more talented 'gators like Matthew, ideally ones with broad knowledge and experience in the parts of the world where they work, with fluency in local languages and dialects, and with a subtle understanding of what makes people tick.

Because if you know that, you also know what makes them talk.

PART I
PROLOGUE

By God, your dreams will be defeated by our blood and by our bodies. What is coming is even worse.

—ABU MUSAB AL ZARQAWI

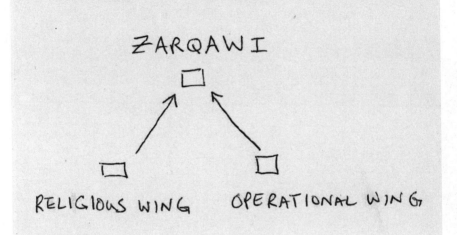

THE GOLDEN DOME

MARCH, 2006

THERE'S A JOKE interrogators like to tell: "What's the difference between a 'gator and a used car salesman?" Answer: "A 'gator has to abide by the Geneva Conventions."

We 'gators don't hawk Chevys; we sell hope to prisoners and find targets for shooters. Today, my group of 'gators arrives in Iraq at a time when our country is searching for a better way to conduct sales.

After 9/11, military interrogators focused on two techniques: fear and control. The Army trained their 'gators to confront and dominate prisoners. This led down the disastrous path to the Abu Ghraib scandal. At Guantánamo Bay, the early interrogators not only abused the detainees, they tried to belittle their religious beliefs. I'd heard stories from a friend who had been there that some of the 'gators even tried to convert prisoners to Christianity.

These approaches rarely yielded results. When the media

got wind of what those 'gators were doing, our disgrace was detailed on every news broadcast and front page from New York to Islamabad.

Things are about to change. Traveling inside the bowels of an air force C-130 transport, my group is among the first to bring a new approach to interrogating detainees. Respect, rapport, hope, cunning, and deception are our tools. The old ones—fear and control—are as obsolete as the buggy whip. Unfortunately, not everyone embraces change.

The C-130 sweeps low over mile after mile of nothingness. Sand dunes, flats, red-orange to the horizon are all I can see through my porthole window in the rear of our four-engine ride. It is as desolate as it was in biblical times. Two millenia later, little has changed but the methods with which we kill.

"Never thought I'd be back here again," I remark to my seatmate, Ann. She's a noncommissioned officer (NCO) in her early thirties, a tough competitor and an athlete on the air force volleyball team.

She passes me a handful of M&M's. We've been swapping snacks all through the flight. "When were you here?" she asks, peering out at the desertscape below. Her long blonde hair peeks out from under her Kevlar helmet.

"Three years ago. April of o-three," I reply.

That was a wild ride. I'd been stationed in Saudi Arabia as a counterintelligence agent. A one-day assignment had sent me north to Baghdad, shivering in the back of another C-130 Hercules.

Below us today the southern Iraqi desert looks calm. Nothing moves; the small towns we pass over appear empty. In 2003 it was a different story. We flew in at night, and I

6

watched the remnants of the war go by from 200 feet, a set of night-vision goggles strapped to my head. Tracer bullets and triple A (antiaircraft artillery) arced out of the dark ground past our aircraft, our pilot banking the Herc hard to avoid the barrages. Most of the way north, the night was laced with fire. Yet when we landed at Baghdad International, we found the place eerie and quiet. Burned-out tanks and armored vehicles lay broken around the perimeter. I later found out they'd been destroyed by marauding A-10 Warthogs.

On this return flight, we face no opposition. The pilots fly low and smooth. The cargo section of these C-130's is always cold. I pop the M&M's into my mouth and fold my arms across my chest. The engines beat a steady cadence as the C-130 shivers and bucks. Ann puts her iPod's buds in her ears and closes her eyes. Next to her, I start to doze.

An hour later, I wake up. A quick check out of the porthole reveals the sprawl of Baghdad below. We cross the Tigris River, and I see one of Saddam's former palaces that I'd seen in '03.

"We're getting close," I say to Ann.

She removes her earbuds.

"What?" she asks.

Mike, another agent in my group, leans in from across the aisle to join our conversation. He offers me beef jerky, and I take a piece.

"We're getting close," I repeat myself.

We reach our destination, a base north of Baghdad. The C-130 swings into the pattern and within minutes, the pilots paint the big transport onto the runway. We taxi for a little while, then swing into a parking space. The pilots cut the engines. The ramp behind us drops, and I see several enlisted men step inside the bird to grab our bags. Each of us brought five duffels plus our gun cases. When we walk, we look like two-legged baggage carts.

"Welcome to the war," somebody says behind me.

After hours of those big turboprops churning away, all is quiet. We descend from the side door just aft of the cockpit. As we hit the tarmac, a bus drives up. A female civilian contractor jumps out and says, "Okay, load up!"

Just as I find a seat on the bus I hear a dull thump, like somebody's just slammed a door in a nearby building—except there aren't any nearby buildings.

A siren starts to wail.

"Oh my God!" screams our driver. "Mortars!"

She stands up from behind the wheel and dives for the nearly closed door, where she promptly gets stuck. Half-in, half-out of the bus she screams, "Mortars! Mortars!"

We look on with wry smiles.

Another dull thud echoes in the distance. The driver flies into a panic. "Get to the bunkers now! Bunkers! Move!" She finally extricates herself from the door and I see her running at high speed down the tarmac.

"Shall we?" I ask Ann.

"Better than waiting for her to come back."

We get off the bus and lope after our driver. We watch her head into a long concrete shelter and we follow and duck inside behind her. It is pitch black.

Another thump. This one seems closer. The ground shakes a little.

It is very dark in here. The bunker is more like a long, U-shaped tunnel. I can't help but think about bugs and spiders. This would be their Graceland.

"Watch out for camel spiders," I say to Ann. She's still next to me.

"What's a camel spider?" she asks.

"A big, aggressive desert spider," says a nearby voice. I can't see who said that, but I recognize the voice. It is Mike, our Cajun. Back home he's a lawyer and a former police sniper. He's a fit thirty-year-old civilian agent obsessed with tactical gear.

"How big?" Ann asks dubiously. She's not sure if we're pulling her leg. We're not.

"About as big as your hand," I say.

"I hear they can jump three feet high," says Steve. He's a thirty-year-old NCO and another agent in our group of air force investigators-turned-interrogators. This tall, buzz-cut adrenaline junkie from the Midwest likes racing funny cars in his spare time. In the States, his cockiness was suspect. Out here, I wonder if it won't be exactly what we need.

"Seriously?" Ann asks.

Thump! The bunker shivers. Another mortar has landed. This one even closer.

"I'm still more worried about the spiders," Mike says.

I have visions of a camel spider scuttling across my boot. I look down, but it's so dark that I can't even see my feet.

The all-clear signal sounds. We file out of the bunker and make our way back to the bus. The driver tails us, looking haggard and embarrassed. Her panic attack cost her whatever respect we could have for her. We climb aboard her bus and she takes us to our next stop.

We "inprocess," waiting in line for the admin types to stamp our paperwork. We have no idea what's taking them so long. Hurry up. Wait. Hurry up. Wait. It's the rhythm of the military.

Steve finishes first and walks over to us. "Hey, one of the admin guys just told me a mortar round landed right around the corner and killed a soldier."

The news is like cold water. Any thought of complaining about the wait dies on our tongues. We'd been cavalier about the attack. Now it seems real.

A half hour passes before we are processed. Our driver shows up with the first sergeant and shuttles us across the base to the Special Forces compound where we'll stay until we accomplish our mission (whatever that is).

When I went home in June, 2003, I thought the war was over—mission accomplished—but it had just changed form. We've arrived in Iraq near the war's third anniversary. The army, severely stretched between two wars and short of personnel, has reached out to the other services for help. Our small group was handpicked by the air force to go to Iraq as interrogators to assist our brothers in green. We volunteered not knowing what we'd be doing or where. Some of us thought we'd go to Afghanistan, perhaps joining the hunt for Osama bin Laden. Only at the last minute before we left the States did we find out where we were going. We still don't know our mission, but we've been told it has the highest priority.

We're all special agents and experienced criminal investigators for the air force. One of us is a civilian agent and the rest of us are military. I'm the only officer. Ever since the Abu Ghraib fiasco, the army has struggled in searching for new ways to extract information from detainees. We offer an alternative approach. In the weeks to come, we'll try to prove our new techniques work, but if we cross the wrong people, we'll be sent home. They told us that much before we left for the sandbox.

Later that night, after stashing our bags in our trailer homes, we sit in the interrogation unit's briefing room down the hall from the commander's office. ████████████

████████████████████████████████████

████████████████████████

My agents are called one by one into the commander's office for an evaluation. All of them pass. Finally, a tall, black-haired Asian-American man with a bushy black beard steps into the briefing room. "Matthew?" he says to me.

I step forward. He regards me and says, "I'm David, the senior interrogator." He leads me to the commander's office and follows me inside.

"Have a seat," David says.

I look around. There's only one free chair, a plush, over-stuffed leather number next to one of the desks, so I settle into it.

The office is cramped, made even more claustrophobic by two large desks squatting in opposite corners. Behind one is a gruff-looking sergeant major. David sits next to the door. A third man watches me intently from the far corner, and the interrogation unit commander, Roger, sits behind a desk to my right.

Everyone else sitting in the room is in ergonomic hell. I feel uneasy as I take the best seat in the house. Roger explains to me that this is an informal board designed to make sure we'd be a good fit for the interrogation unit. "We're going to ask you some questions."

I struggle to sit up. The chair has me in a comfy grip. If

I'm about to be grilled, this is the last chair I want to be in. I finally have to sit forward, back rigid, to find a position that doesn't make me look like an overrelaxed flake.

"Look," Roger says, "We're happy to have you here."

"Glad to be here."

"Okay, let's get started. David, do you want to go first?"

"Sure," he says. He has dark rings under both eyes.

"Tell me, what countries border Iraq?" David asks.

"Turkey to the north. Iran to the east, Saudi Arabia and Kuwait to the south, Jordan and Syria to the west." I answer. My mind races. Did I miss anything between Syria and Turkey?

"Okay. What's the difference between Shia and Sunni?"

That's an easy one. "It goes back to the schism in Islam caused by the death of Muhammad. Sunnis believe that the legitimate successor was Muhammad's closest disciple, Abu Bakr. Shia believe the succession should have been passed through his cousin Ali, who was also his daughter Fatima's husband. The Shia lost, and Abu Bakr retained leadership until he died."

David, thinking I'm finished, starts to ask something else. Before he can, I continue, "When Abu Bakr died, the Shia tried to recapture the leadership of Islam, but Ali's son Hussein was murdered outside Karbala, and the Sunnis have held the balance of power ever since."

"What the fuck makes you think you can do this job?" It is the sergeant major.

"I'm a criminal investigator and I interrogated on the criminal side. Plus I've worked with Saudis so I understand the culture."

He doesn't look mollified. "You're a major, right?" he almost sneers when he says my rank.

"Yes."

"Around here, there is no rank. We are on a first-name basis. If some young sergeant ends up giving you orders, are you going to have a hard ███████ time with that?"

"I never confuse competence with rank," I reply.

███████ A," the sergeant major says.

The man in the far corner steps up to the plate. "I'm Doctor Brady. I want to know if you consider yourself bright enough for this job. You're going to be interrogating Al Qaida leaders and men much older than you. What makes you think you can outsmart them?"

"I don't have to outsmart them," I say. "*We'll* have to outsmart them. I know there'll be a team of analysts supporting me."

We've come full circle. Roger takes the stage and asks, "If you saw somebody, say an interpreter, threatening a detainee, what would you do?"

"I'd make him stop."

"What if you only suspect he's threatening the detainee in Arabic and it's helping your interrogation?"

"I'd pull him aside and ask him what's going on. If he didn't stop, I'd bring it up with you."

"How do you feel about waterboarding, or other enhanced interrogation techniques?"

Ah, the heart of the matter. Ever since Abu Ghraib everyone in the interrogation business has been on edge. Careers are at stake. Jail time is at stake.

"I'm opposed to enhanced techniques. They're against

Geneva Conventions and, ultimately, they do more harm than good. Besides we don't need them."

"What do you mean?"

"A good interrogator can get the information he needs in more subtle ways," I reply.

"Okay," Roger says dismissively, "Wait outside. We need to talk."

Ten minutes later, I'm called back in. Roger smiles and shakes my hand. "Welcome aboard. Get ready because everything will come at you fast. Rule number one: we have a no-tolerance policy for violations of Geneva Conventions. You'll sit in on three interrogations to see how we do things, then you'll be on your own."

David adds, "By the way, do you have any leadership experience?"

"That's pretty much what I do," I reply.

"Good," Roger says. "In three weeks, we're going to need a new senior interrogator. You're it."

Laughter erupts around the room. Apparently, this is a job nobody wants. Looking at David, I think I can understand why.

"It means longer hours," David tells me.

"Whatever it takes."

"Good. We're about to have our twenty-three hundred meeting. Come with us and learn. Then grab some sleep. You'll start first thing in the morning."

I follow David, Roger, the sergeant major, and the doc down the hall to a briefing room. Here the entire interrogation unit is gathered. As we walk in, David says to me, "We've got interrogators and analysts here. The analysts brief us before every interrogation. They tell us what they want to get from each detainee. Got it?"

"Sure."

"It'll be your job to get the stuff they need. How you do it will be up to you."

David goes to sit at the head table, and I find a seat next to Mike and my group of agents at the back of the room. In the front of the room is a rectangular table with the interrogation unit's leadership—the commander, the senior interrogator, the senior analyst, the doc, the admin guy, and the operations officer. The ops officer is a short stocky guy with a neatly trimmed beard named Randy who looks like Rob Thomas, the floppy-haired lead singer of Matchbox Twenty. He runs the meeting. Each of the interrogators and analysts take turns discussing the detainees as their faces appear on a large flat-screen television in front of us. Randy lays out the priorities for the next shift, then talks about what's been discovered from the previous one. Toward the end of the meeting, a colonel walks into the room.

Someone next to us says, "That's the task force commander. Veteran of the Battle of Mogadishu, which *Black Hawk Down* was based on."

He's charismatic enough to have played himself in the movie. He has short black hair and an athletic build and he walks with a casual confidence. His voice is low and deliberate. It's obvious that he is a man of few words.

"Ladies and gentlemen," he begins. "I'm proud of what you've accomplished so far. I see how hard you work and I know you will achieve success. Right now, though, we need to pick up the pace."

He pauses. The colonel is a natural orator. "You have the toughest job in the country."

It strikes me that we don't know what our new job is, besides interrogating detainees and getting information.

The colonel reveals it. "For you new guys, here's a run-down. Last month, Al Qaida blew up the Golden Dome Mosque in Samarra. This was a Shia shrine—one of their holiest. To a Catholic it'd be like blowing up the Sistine Chapel."

He lets that sink in. "The destruction of the Golden Dome Mosque has prompted a surge in sectarian violence. Al Qaida's leader here in Iraq, Abu Musab al Zarqawi, has made it his mission to spark a civil war between Sunni and Shia. From now on, you have only one objective: find Zarqawi and kill him before he can do that. Everyone is counting on you."

He turns and strides out of the room.

We've just joined the hunt for the most wanted man in Iraq.

One

THE 'GATOR PIT

DAY 4

Y ALARM RINGS at 0930. I've been in a near-coma after the crazed pace of the past three days, and only the alarm's persistence forces me awake. A few eyeblinks, a long stretch, and I sit up on the edge of my cot. The air conditioner has been rattling all night long, leaving the trailer nice and chilly. Outside, I'm sure the temperature has already broken a hundred and ten.

On my feet, I yawn. We run on a strange schedule here, and it'll take a few more days before I'm used to it. Eleven in the morning to midnight is the nominal shift, but the truth is, to get all the work done we need to get in an hour early and stay two or three hours late. There are no days off.

I grab my shaving kit and head for the shower trailers. The moment my flip-flops hit the sand out in front of my hooch, the heat assails me. The air is still and hot, a jarring transition from the arctic climate of the trailer. This is worse than Saudi and worse than the hottest day I spent while stationed in Arizona. I think of Lawrence of Arabia crossing the Empty Quarter. I don't know how the ground-pounders do it.

I've just started the long walk to the shower trailers when thunder splits the silence. The ground quakes. My hooch rattles behind me. The din swells as I watch a pair of F-16 fighter jets streak past a few hundred meters away.

My trailer sits near the runway and directly below the aircraft traffic pattern. The helicopter parking ramp is a football field away and closer than that is a shooting range. I hear rounds clipping off in my sleep. But none of this can match the CRAM, the antimortar gun. When the insurgents launch mortars, the CRAM launches a barrage of lead to intercept them. It's the loudest, fastest machine gun on earth and it's fifty feet from my trailer. No one sleeps through it.

Throttles open, the F-16s nose up and race for altitude as they tuck away their landing gear. Their thunder recedes, and for a moment the silence of the morning returns. Before I've taken another step for the shower trailer, I get buzzed by a quartet of Blackhawk helicopters. They nestle down on the ramp across from my hooch and cut their engines in unison.

Special Forces (SF) guys are returning from a mission spawned by the intelligence we've elicited. We have a vested interest in being accurate because their lives are at stake every time they climb aboard those choppers. Besides, the SF guys get very unhappy if we send them down a dry hole, or into a trap.

A pair of helicopters skim past next. ████████████
██

The soldiers ride ████████████████████████████
██████████████████████████ into battle sideways, legs
dangling over the skids, ready to cut loose and jump off the
moment the helicopter hits sand.

Just as I reach the shower trailer, the warning siren sounds.
As it wails, two, three . . . finally four bombs fall in the distance. Eighty-two-millimeter mortars, the insurgents' morning greeting, land somewhere on the base far from me. After
three days we're already accustomed to this ritual. We don't
even bother to head for the shelters anymore.

I shower and shave and get dressed for the day. Interrogators wear civilian clothes. Our detainees don't need to
know our rank or branch of the military. Besides, it fosters
an egalitarian atmosphere in our office, which is known as
the 'gator pit.

Most of the 'gators have grown beards, and I've already
joined in the fun. Between the beards and the civilian clothes,
we look more like a Berkeley-based think tank than an elite
military unit on a critical mission.

The first three days have been a whirlwind, and the learning curve is steep. We read thick three-ring binders full of
policies and procedures; then we're given the latest intelligence briefings. The star of the briefings is our target, Abu
Musab al Zarqawi, the leader of Al Qaida in Iraq.

Born in Jordan, Zarqawi started life as a common street
thug who served time in a Jordanian jail for sexual assault
before he found Islam. While in prison, he embraced funda-
mentalism. Once released, he traveled to Afghanistan, where

he joined Osama bin Laden in the jihad against the Soviet Union.

When that war ended, he returned to Jordan and planned terrorist acts to bring down the government. When his operations failed and the authorities closed in on him, he fled to Afghanistan in 2001 and rejoined bin Laden, though his relationship with the master terrorist seems to have been tenuous. Osama reportedly thought Zarqawi little more than an uneducated stooge.

Before the American invasion, Zarqawi moved to northern Iraq to develop a new terrorist network called Tawhid al Jihad. He established strong ties all over Sunni Iraq, which proved pivotal for Al Qaida after the American attack in 2003. Thanks to this preparation, Zarqawi's group was able to launch lethal and attention-grabbing attacks starting in the summer of 2003. He bombed the United Nations headquarters in Baghdad's Green Zone. His minions also bombed the Jordanian Embassy and three Western hotels in Amman, Jordan.

His group became the masters of suicide bombings. Instead of targeting Americans or other Coalition military personnel, Zarqawi's true believers went after helpless Shia civilians. They blew up market places. Suicide bombers detonated themselves inside cafés or other crowded everyday targets.

Why kill innocent Muslim civilians? Zarqawi had a plan. He wanted to exploit the centuries-old division between Shia and Sunni to create a civil war inside Iraq. Such a conflict could only bog down American troops and ensnare the United States in a protracted conflict. His plan worked brilliantly.

His successes gained him the respect of bin Laden, and he swore *bayat* (allegiance) to Al Qaida and became Al Qaida's chief for Mesopotamia.

During one of our briefings, we are shown a video of Al Qaida terrorists dressed in black standing in front of a seated Nicholas Berg, the American contractor who was kidnapped in Iraq.

A terrorist wearing a black mask slices Berg's throat with a knife. Berg dies horribly. The terrorists seem unfazed. Our briefer tells us the man with the knife is Abu Musab al Zarqawi himself. Not only does he order people to commit acts of carnage; he has the blood of innocents on his own hands.

If we can find Zarqawi and capture or kill him, our intelligence community believes we can stop the suicide bombings. Stop the suicide bombings and the Sunni-on-Shia civil war will end. We can stabilize Iraq and save countless innocent lives if only we can stop Zarqawi and his organization.

At the end of our briefings, we are told that Zarqawi is now a higher priority than Osama bin Laden himself.

On my first day, David teams me up with a veteran 'gator named Mary. She's a short haired Asian-American woman in her late twenties who used to work for nonprofits. Now she's a contract interrogator for the Department of Defense. She teaches me the administrative side of the house, such as report formats and how to sign out detainees, and I sit through six interrogations with her.

The interrogation booth is nothing more than a bare six-by-six room with plywood walls, plastic chairs, and a table. There's a high-definition flat-screen TV on one wall that is hooked up to a laptop on the table with all the latest maps and imagery of Iraq. We use those to mark targets whenever the detainee gives one up.

What I learn from Mary during those first six interrogations matches what we were taught at the schoolhouse, the name we use to describe our six-week interrogation training course at Fort Huachuca, Arizona. Because everyone in my group of interrogators has been a criminal investigator, we went through a fire-hose version of the five-month interrogation school.

Mary runs the approved approaches based on fear and control, as we were taught. An *approach* is 'gator-speak for a tactic contrived to convince a detainee to offer information. There are a dozen of them in the army manual that we used for training. For instance, "Love of Family" is an approach where an interrogator tries to get a detainee to cooperate out of love for his family and a desire to return to them. Mary runs the approaches adeptly, but none of her detainees provides useful information.

The techniques I've observed so far are quite different from what we used in criminal interrogations back home in the States. When I worked as a criminal interrogator, we focused on methods based on understanding and cooperation, not control.

Today, my fourth day in country, I will be assigned to a new partner named Bobby.

More choppers come and go as I hike the half-mile red-sand trail to our hangar-turned-office. A C-130 roars by, followed a few minutes later by a beefy-looking C-17 jet transport. My new home is on the edge of the Middle Eastern O'Hare International.

At 1015, I step into the 'gator pit. The central hub for our operation, it is a big bull-pen office area filled with long tables, desks, chairs, and computers. The tables are scuffed and most of the chairs are broken. A layer of powdery dust covers everything and gives the place the look of an office at the end of the world.

I share a long table with Doc Brady. On my first day here, I noticed that somehow he'd scored the best chair in the house. Today, his leather high-back is missing, replaced by a rusted and bent metal folding chair. I sit down next to it and notice the whiteboard at the front of the 'gator pit. It lists all the assignments for the day, but every morning somebody puts up a little witticism about our operations officer, Randy. Randy is an ex–Special Forces officer turned intelligence guru who is titanium-tough and has devoted the last three years of his life to chasing Zarqawi.

The whiteboard reads: *When Randy wants vegetables, he eats a vegetarian.*

As I'm chuckling over this, Doc Brady arrives. He looks down at his new chair, and his bald head turns a surprising shade of crimson.

"Matthew," he says through taut lips, "where did my chair go?"

"It was missing when I got here, Doc," I reply.

I've already learned that he appreciates formalities and does not have much of a sense of humor. This makes him the butt of many jokes.

Annoyed, he heads off in search of his chair.

"Matthew," I hear a voice behind me.

When I turn around, I see Bobby. "Remember something, okay? Good chairs are currency around here. Like good cigarettes."

He chuckles and nods over at the doctor's chair.

Bobby is in his early twenties, an enlisted man in the army and a corn-fed boy from Nebraska.

He extends his arm and gives me a firm handshake.

"Glad to be working with you," he says.

"I'm here to learn," I reply.

"Well, I think we'll be learning from each other. When we get in the booth, don't be afraid to ask questions, okay?"

"Great." This is encouraging.

"Hey, did I hear you used to fly helicopters?" Bobby asks.

"Yeah. MH-53s. Pave Lows."

"I flew King Airs back home before I joined the army."

This is getting better. We're two aviators working together. I'm starting to get my hopes up.

"When I was flying King Airs . . ." Bobby starts.

Our operations officer interrupts him.

"Eleven hundred, people, let's go."

Meeting time. We shuffle toward the conference room. As we go, Bobby leans into me, "We'll talk more later."

Across the 'gator pit, Doc Brady discovers his chair. He pushes it back to our table and eyes Bobby suspiciously as we walk by. Bobby barely conceals a grin.

The meeting lasts about an hour. Randy lays out the priorities for the day and gives us some direction. When we break up, Bobby leads me back out to the 'gator pit. "Let's go find Cliff," he tells me.

"Who's Cliff?"

"He's our übernerd."

I can't help but laugh. Bobby continues, "He's the Bill Gates of our analyst staff. The guy works nonstop and he's got a brilliant mind. He's just a little bit socially awkward. He'll give us a list of objectives and questions to ask during the interrogation."

We pass through the 'gator pit. As we walk past my table, Bobby lets out a surprised, "Holy shit. . . . Look what the Doc's done!"

I follow Bobby's gaze and see Doc Brady's empty leather chair handcuffed to the table leg.

"That'll teach whoever's stealing it," I manage through the laughter.

"Nah, now it's a challenge," Bobby grins.

As we're admiring the doc's ingenuity, Cliff approaches. Bobby introduces us and says, "Okay, we've got Abu Ali and Zaydan today, Cliff. What are we looking for?"

Cliff wears a pair of John Lennon–style glasses that keep slipping down his nose. He pushes them up absently as he explains, "They're both from the religious wing. We need to find out who their boss is. Failing that, get the location of more safe houses."

"Religious wing?" I ask.

Cliff nods as he hands a list of questions over to Bobby. "Yes. Al Qaida is broken into two branches here in Iraq. The religious wing operates out of mosques and is in charge of recruiting and financing. The operational wing carries out attacks. Zaydan and Abu Ali fit into the religious side of the house."

They didn't teach us any of that back in the States.

"Zaydan was caught a few weeks ago," Bobby tells me. "Oh, Cliff, you gotta tell Matthew about the kid in the van."

A shy smile forms on Cliff's face. "Well, Zaydan and Abu Ali are childhood friends. Bobby got Zaydan to give up a safe house in Yusufiyah . . ."

"That's an area south of Baghdad," Bobby interrupts.

"Al Qaida utilizes a series of at least a dozen safe houses around that area. They rotate them all the time. Zaydan probably thought the house would be empty."

"Except it wasn't," Bobby says triumphantly.

"Except it wasn't," Cliff agrees.

They both start laughing.

"What?" I ask.

"The Special Forces team hit the target house. Out in front was a van, and as they approached, they could see people inside." Cliff starts to blush.

"When they opened the back door, they found a nineteen-year-old boy having relations with a fifteen-year-old girl."

"Having relations?" Bobby asks. "Cliff, come on! You gotta tell the story better than that!"

"Sorry," he mumbles.

"So look," Bobby says, "the SF team assaults the car, right? When they rip open the doors, weapons ready, there're these two kids gettin' their groove on."

Now I'm laughing. Cliff blushes bright pink.

Bobby continues, "The SF guys didn't know what to do at first. You know how the girl's family would have reacted, right?"

"Premarital sex?" I say. "They would have been shamed."

Bobby nods in agreement. "They would've beaten the

shit out of her. Fucking Iraqis. God I hate this fucking place"

"Anyway," he says, "the SF guys let them go. The boy's probably scarred for life."

"And the girl, too," Cliff notes.

"So at the same time the other members of the team hit the house and they find Abu Ali inside. He'd been blessing suicide bombers there, but by the time the SF guys arrived, the bombers were long gone."

"Into Baghdad," says Cliff.

"Yeah. Probably blowing up some Shia marketplace."

"Zaydan ends up ratting out his best friend and not even knowing it. That's the best part."

"Does Abu Ali know that?" I ask.

"No. And we won't tell him either. But they know they're both locked up here," says Bobby.

"It isn't a good idea to reveal that information," Cliff tells me. "Once we're done with them here, they go to Abu Ghraib. If they know somebody sold them out, they'll try to kill them. Besides, they interrogate them over there, too. Information like that could cause a detainee to stop cooperating."

"I understand," I say.

I think back to the lesson at the schoolhouse: never make a promise you can't keep because you'll burn your bridge.

"Okay, let's go grab some chow; then we'll get started. Whaddya say?" Bobby asks.

"Sounds like a plan."

"Besides, I'm dying for a Coke. I need my caffeine fix."

I shudder to think what Bobby's going to be like with a

boatload of caffeine in him. I make a mental note to keep him away from energy drinks.

We say good-bye to Cliff and head off for the mess hall. As we go, Bobby slaps me on the back and starts in again, "So there I was in my King Air 300 . . ."

It's going to be a good day.

Two

THE SKELETON

THE JOVIALITY AND comradeship of the morning long forgotten, I sit beside Bobby in front of a human skeleton. It is Abu Ali, a Sunni. His orange prison jumpsuit sags off him like he's a bony coat hangar. Bitterness seems to leech out of him. This man is my introduction to Al Qaida in Iraq.

Our interpreter, Hadir, stands in the far left corner behind Abu Ali. The 'terp looks reluctant to speak.

Bobby glances at Hadir, though we're generally supposed to maintain eye contact with our detainee. "What did he say?"

Hadir frowns. Then, in a perfect mimic of Abu Ali's tone, says, "You came to my country, to Iraq. You Americans ruined our lives and now you want to help me?"

Bobby nods. "Yes, Abu Ali, we can help you. Don't you want to see your family again? Your wife and daughter? Help us to help you."

He does not reply. Bobby decides to press on. "I know we've been through this before. Who did you work for?"

No answer. He stares unblinking at us.

Bobby had warned me beforehand that Abu Ali is a hard case. He hasn't given anything up, despite numerous interrogations. At the same time, he's not afraid to be direct, especially when it comes to his hatred for Americans.

Bobby turns to me and says, "See, I'm telling you this guy is something else. Go ahead, ask him what he'd do if you gave him a knife."

My attention returns to our detainee. "Abu Ali, what would you do if I gave you a knife?"

"I would slit your throat and watch you die."

His gaze on me is even. He doesn't blink. His hands never move from his lap, where they are folded. He is a statue.

"See," says Bobby to me, "this fucking guy is unbelievable."

I ask the next question. "You mean just because I'm an American, you would kill me now if you could? Even though I mean you no harm?"

"I would kill you. You Americans robbed us of everything."

Abu Ali says something else. Hadir translates again, "You created this hell that we are living in."

Bobby ignores the comment and changes the subject. "Abu Ali, why don't you tell my new team member Matthew why you joined Al Qaida?"

"Certainly," he responds, as I marvel at his self-possession.

He'd be an amazing poker player if he could just hide his eyes. His eyes are his "tell"—they give him away.

"It goes back to when you Americans first invaded Iraq," he begins. His lips barely move. He doesn't even seem to be breathing.

"At that time, I lived in southern Baghdad. I was an imam at our local mosque. Everyone lived happily together— Sunni and Shia, we lived in peace."

I doubt the Shia would see it that way, given what Saddam did to them for years, but I make no comment, nor do I give anything away with body language. Interrogating is acting. You hide yourself away and present whatever façade encourages the detainee to volunteer information.

He continues in a monotone, "Sunni and Shia lived as neighbors. My mother is Shia. She converted to Sunni when she married my father. There was harmony."

"What happened after the invasion?" I ask.

"You Americans removed Saddam. We lost our protection. America doesn't care about Sunnis. You let the Shia militias kill my people."

I've studied the Badr Corps. They're Ayatollah Ali al Sistani's Shia street army. They're ruthless and well organized.

"Which Shia militias?" I ask.

As Hadir translates this, I notice he's started to get fidgety. We've only been in the booth for about twenty minutes. Bobby set the air conditioner on the lowest setting, and it is chilly in here, but that doesn't explain Hadir's behavior.

"The Badr Corps. The Madhi Army. There are many militias."

"What do they want?"

"They want power. Dominance. They want to kill us and drive us from our homes."

And they want revenge for the hundreds of thousands of Shia who died under Saddam's rule. The tyrant's gone and now, right under our nose, the Shia are avenging those deaths.

"I owned a clothing store," Abu Ali continues, "One day, I came to the store and found a note. The note read 'Pack your things and leave. You have forty-eight hours or you will die.' The bottom of the page had the symbol of the Badr Corps."

He lets that sink in. We stare at each other. Bobby doesn't blink. Neither do I.

"What did you do?" I ask.

"I would have stayed. This was my home. My shop. I loved my mosque. But the next morning I learned the Badr Corps had killed a friend of mine, who was also an imam. He lived in the neighborhood next to mine."

His face hardens. His thin lips tighten into a frown. "I did what I had to do to save my family. We packed up and moved back to my hometown in Yusufiyah. I lost my shop. My livelihood. The Badr Corps took it over."

It is hard not to feel sympathy for this man, despite his malignance. He is clearly traumatized. But we have to figure out how to use his trauma to our advantage.

"I returned to the mosque of my childhood. It was there I met fellow Sunni willing to stand and fight for our people."

"Did you volunteer to help?" I ask.

"No. They recruited me."

I lean forward in my chair. I try to act earnest and sympathetic. "Abu Ali, why Al Qaida? Why not one of the Sunni groups like Ansar al Sunna or the 1920 Revolution Brigades?"

Hadir translates this, then cracks a Coke. As he takes a long pull from it, he watches Abu Ali's response.

"There were not any left in Yusufiyah. You Americans wiped them out. We had no access to money or weapons. Without Al Qaida, we had nothing."

That's the first time I've heard this. Is he lying?

"I did not know it was Al Qaida at first."

This is bullshit. He had to have suspected. I need to call him on this.

"Come on, Abu Ali, you must have known."

"Not at first," he insists. Bobby watches him, stone-faced. He doesn't believe this either.

"But when I found out, it was not important. We needed weapons, they gave them to us."

"So you believe in Al Qaida's goals?"

Abu Ali stares hard at me, sizing me up. He says nothing for a moment.

"No, I am Iraqi. I only want back my home."

Bobby cuts in, "Tell Matthew what you did for Al Qaida."

The moment is broken. Abu Ali's eyes flick to Bobby. Then he shifts in his chair and looks over at Hadir.

"Don't fucking look at him. I asked you the question. Show some respect," Bobby orders. He sounds firm— perhaps overly so. He's the youngest one in the room and seems to be compensating a little. He wants Abu Ali to know who's in control. Abu Ali turns his head and engages Bobby. They say nothing. The stare-down goes on for thirty seconds.

Abu Ali cracks first. "I recruited," he says at last.

"How?" I ask. His attention shifts to me.

"I preached at the mosque. I urged my fellow Sunni to join the struggle. If we did not fight, you Americans would let the Shia destroy us."

"Tell Matthew what else you did," Bobby prompts.

Abu Ali nods and continues in that preternaturally calm voice.

"Later, I was told to go to a house out in the countryside. I did not know why. When I arrived, I found I was to bless some of our men before they left for their missions."

"What sort of missions?" I ask.

For just an instant, a flicker of doubt appears on his face. His voice drops to almost a whisper, "Martyrs."

"You were blessing suicide bombers?"

"Yes." He shifts in his chair, the first movement I've seen from him.

He's uncomfortable with this. I want to find out why.

"You blessed them?"

Again a pause. He averts his eyes. I notice he's staring at the floor now.

I look over at Bobby. I want to ask more questions, but Bobby is the lead 'gator here, and I also want to make sure I'm not stepping on his turf. His expression is open. *Have at it.*

"Did you believe in this tactic?"

Abu Ali replies slowly, "Not . . . at . . . first."

"What made you change your mind?"

He mumbles a response. Hadir asks him to repeat his answer.

His eyes go icy. He pulls into himself, drawing his shoulders forward and folding his arms across his boyish frame.

34

His dark skin is taught across his bones. Whatever is inside this man is eating him alive.

He repeats his answer, but his voice is so soft that Hadir still can't understand.

Abu Ali clenches his teeth and bares a caustic smile. His third answer is clipped, firm, and loud.

Hadir mimics it perfectly. "You Americans left us no choice. Suicide bombers are our only defense."

Bobby jumps in. "What do you mean?"

"Our only hope is to cause civil war. Then other Sunnis will come here to help us."

His chin rises. Defiantly he adds, "I did what I had to do."

I decide to let him play victim.

"The martyrs killed *Shia*," he says. "The Shia deserved to die." He sounds like he's talking about exterminating bugs.

"And you are proud of that?" I ask.

"Yes. I am proud."

I detect a slight waver in his voice. Is he posturing? Or is he bitter that he has allowed himself to become an imam who supported mass murder?

"This is what you want for the future? This is the Iraq you want to give to your daughter?"

"It is the only way we will survive." His voice takes on an edge.

I'll remember this sore spot for later.

Bobby begins to flick his pen against his notebook. It beats a steady rhythm into the silence. I get up and turn down the AC.

Bobby takes the lead.

"You know Abu Ali, we're talking with Zaydan."

Abu Ali stares placidly at Bobby.

"If Zaydan talks first, we will make a deal with him. He will go home to his family. You will stand trial at Abu Ghraib. Do you know what the punishment is for those caught aiding suicide bombers?"

"Death."

His voice is flat and devoid of emotion. Yet his body language screams hate.

"That does not have to be your fate, Abu Ali," Bobby answers. "If you tell us what we want to know, we will go to the judges on your behalf. There's one American, one Shia, and one Sunni. We can put in a good word for you, maybe change the American's mind and the Sunni's mind."

Abu Ali looks unmoved.

"We can convince them you are an asset who is helping us. Maybe you do a little time at Abu Ghraib, hang out with your friends, and go home," Bobby says earnestly. His face is open and honest. Given what he said about hating Iraqis and Iraq earlier, I'm surprised at his expression. I find myself almost believing him.

"Help us save you," he almost beseeches.

Abu Ali sits in silence. He face gives up nothing.

"Zaydan is already talking," Bobby says, ratcheting up the pressure.

Back in the world of criminal investigation, we call this approach the Prisoner's Dilemma. It's designed to get one guy to turn on another. Tell both the first to talk gets the deal while the other gets the noose, and generally it isn't long before somebody talks.

"I don't care," Abu Ali replies.

"We want to help you, Abu Ali, but we can't do it unless you give us something," Bobby says.

No answer. Abu Ali continues to stare malevolently at us.

"Okay, I think we're done here," Bobby says. He turns to me.

"Actually, I've got another question," I say.

"Go for it."

"Abu Ali, I do not understand your name. Doesn't it mean 'father of Ali?' Yet you only have a daughter."

"It is just a nickname," he replies dismissively.

"Isn't Ali a Shia name?"

"I already told you that my mother was Shia."

"Do you have a nephew that you've taken in?" I ask. That would explain why he's nicknamed Father of Ali.

"No. It is just my wife and daughter in my house."

"How did you get this nickname?"

"It is just a nickname. My mother gave it to me."

His voice is butter smooth, but I think I see a trace of nervousness on his face. If I did, it didn't last long.

I nod to Bobby, indicating I'm finished.

"Okay, we're done for today," Bobby says. "Go back to your cell and think about it, Abu Ali. Think about your family. Put on your mask."

As Abu Ali puts the black mask over his face, Hadir exits to retrieve a guard. A minute later a guard enters and handcuffs Abu Ali's hands behind his back. Hadir bolts from the booth as the guard leads our detainee back to his cell.

After Hadir leaves, I ask, "What's up with our 'terp?"

Bobby points at the door.

"Hadir? Oh, he's a chain-smoker. Leave him in a booth

too long, and he starts to get the shakes. That's why he guzzles those Cokes."

"He didn't hide how much he hates Abu Ali."

"Yeah. Used to be Pershmerga—Kurdish Special Forces. He's got plenty of reason to hate Sunnis."

Bobby slides his notebook under one arm and changes the subject. "Well, what did you think of Abu Ali?"

"That's one cool player. He seems resolved to his fate."

"He doesn't give a damn about anything," Bobby agrees.

That's the worst type of detainee to have. You can't motivate a guy who doesn't care what's going to happen to him. How can you offer a carrot to a horse with no appetite?

Even though I've worked with Bobby for only a few hours, I can sense we've got a good rhythm going.

"We gotta do something to make this guy care," I suggest. "We need to get him emotional. Push his buttons. Even if we just piss him off, we need to move him."

"Yeah, but we need to find the right button to push. I've been looking for a week and haven't found a goddamn thing. I just get nothing from the guy, you know? *Inshallah*, and all that bullshit." Inshallah means "God willing," or "God's will."

Fate plays a major role in Arab societies. In Iraq, I have no doubt many will be like Abu Ali, willing to leave their fate in God's hands. The only way to buck this trend is to go back to the things people hold closest. Family. Pride. Respect. Those things can provoke core emotions and drive up the stakes.

I start thinking out loud. "Draw emotion out of him. That's the way to find what motivates him."

"Bitterness motivates him."

"No, I don't think so. He's bitter over what has become of his life, but I don't think it motivates him."

"It drove him to join Al Qaida."

"Not really," I say, "I think he did that out of self-preservation more than anything else."

"Yeah, probably. Listen, I don't know how to get to this fucking guy. I've run just about every approach in the damn book, and he hasn't cracked. He'll admit to anyone what he's done, but he offers up nothing else."

"How much more time do we have with him?" I ask.

"Not much. At any moment Randy could kick him into Abu Ghraib. I'm not even sure we'll get another shot at him.

"What do we do?"

Bobby thinks it over for a moment. "Let's go pay a visit to Abu Ali's childhood pal. See if we can't work them off each other."

"Do you think they'd rat each other out? They're lifelong friends."

"Probably not, but what do we have to lose?"

Three

THE JOVIAL IMAM

A N HOUR LATER, Bobby and I sit down with Zaydan, Abu Ali's childhood friend. I'm surprised at the difference between the two men. Where Abu Ali is skeletal, Zaydan is rotund. Where Abu Ali is bitter, Zaydan is cheerful. Zaydan exudes no hatred, no poisonous resentment or dislike for Americans. In fact, he doesn't act as if his life hangs in the balance at all.

After Bobby introduces me, he asks Zaydan to explain his role in Al Qaida. Zaydan doesn't hesitate. He freely admits he worked to recruit Sunni fighters through the mosques he preached at in Yusufiyah and southern Baghdad. He joined Al Qaida for the same reasons Abu Ali did. Zarqawi's organization offered him safety from the roving Shia death squads.

In the absence of leadership or structure, the Shia unleashed a wave of vengeance against the Sunnis. They murdered and plundered their way through the Sunni neighborhoods in Baghdad and Najaf, polarizing the population. Our inability to stop the violence drove thousands into Al Qaida's ranks. Zaydan is just one of those, though more important than most since he is an imam.

After Zaydan tells me his story, Bobby goes to work on him. "Zaydan," he begins, "We've been talking for many days now and I'm trying to help you out, but the clock is ticking here. We don't have much time left before you will be transferred to Abu Ghraib. That's no threat, it's just a fact. From here, you'll be sent there to stand trial before three judges."

Zaydan nods dismissively, "I know."

"Okay, then. Help us help you. If you just tell us who your boss is, we can go to the judges and work on your behalf."

"I can't tell you that."

"Why not?"

"I can't."

Bobby glances at me. Though we've only worked together for a few hours, I can already sense what he's thinking. *Can't help because you're loyal to Al Qaida, Zaydan? Or are you afraid of them?*

Bobby tests the waters. "We can protect your family."

Zaydan laughs. His bulging belly rolls with the effort. We stare at him, unsure of what sparked this outburst. Finally, he says, "You Americans already protect my family."

"What are you talking about?"

"My family lives in a compound in Yusufiyah. It is a new settlement, walled and guarded. There is a checkpoint at the entrance. U.S. Marines guard it."

Bobby and I are floored. An elite community in the most actively hostile area outside Anbar Province protects the family of one of Al Qaida's top recruiters in Baghdad.

Bobby makes no effort to hide his surprise. "Really?"

Zaydan laughs and replies, "Sure. Abu Ali's family is there as well!"

I ask, "You mean his wife and daughter?"

Zaydan frowns, "No, his wife, son, and daughter."

Interrogations are like poker games. This sort of revelation is obviously significant. We just can't let our detainee know he's inadvertently given us something of value. I cover up.

"I forgot he had a son."

"Why do you think I call him Abu Ali?" Zaydan chides us. "Abu means 'father of' and his son is named Ali."

The interrogation rolls on, with Bobby working the Love of Family approach. He can't get Zaydan to budge. On the fly, he makes a decision not to use the Prisoner's Dilemma yet on Zaydan. I'll have to ask him about that later.

Two hours later, we've gone in circles. We're no closer to breaking him or finding his motivation. With our troops already protecting his family's home, we have no observable leverage. Bobby ends the interrogation with a resigned, "You know, Zaydan, we're at a standstill. I like you. You're a good guy, and I want to help you. But I don't know what else I can do."

"I am sorry, my friend. I cannot tell you who I work for or where to find him."

And that's that. We end the interrogation. As we walk back to the 'gator pit, I ask Bobby, "So do you think he doesn't trust us? Or is he afraid for his family?"

"Not sure. Maybe both. You can't believe what Al Qaida does to members who turn on them. I'll show you the videos sometime."

"I can imagine," I say.

"No. You can't. Believe me. They use power drills on the squealer's arms and legs. Sometimes on their heads, too."

We reach the pit and report to Cliff what little we learned. He seems disappointed.

"Randy's not going to keep him or Abu Ali around much longer," he tells us. "They're not giving us anything, and the SF guys bring in new catches every night. Sooner or later, they're going to Abu Ghraib."

Bobby agrees, "Probably sooner."

"Hey, why did you decide not to run a Prisoner's Dilemma on Zaydan?" I ask.

"Eh, maybe next time," Bobby says, but I can tell there's something else on his mind.

"Okay, what next?" I ask.

Bobby ponders this. "Well, why do you think Abu Ali hid the fact that he has a son?"

"Weakness?"

"Maybe. Let's ask him first thing tomorrow."

Four

LOVE OF FAMILY

THE NEXT MORNING, we start with Abu Ali. A guard brings him into our interrogation booth. He glares at us as soon as his mask is removed. Hadir, our 'terp, stands to one side, already jonesing for a cigarette. He tries to drown his nicotine habit with liberal slurps of Coke.

Bobby gets right to the point. "You have a son."

Abu Ali doesn't even blink.

"Why didn't you tell us you had a son?"

His lips curl into a semismile. It suits him about as much as a pink collar on a junkyard dog.

"You caught me," he says.

He sits back, the semismile stamped on his face. He was hiding a weakness.

"How old is your son?"

The semismile evaporates. He growls something that Hadir translates as "Eleven years old. He is just a boy."

This gives me an idea. I glance at Bobby who tips his head in another *go for it* gesture.

"Your family is staying near Zaydan's family, right?"

Abu Ali shuffles in his chair at this question and doesn't answer.

"They are under the protection of our marines. Why did you move them there?"

"Because it is safe."

"So isn't there a way for us to work together to make Iraq safer?" I say.

Abu Ali answers me with silence and a stare.

"Abu Ali, think about your son. What will happen to him in this Iraq?"

Implacable silence greets my question, but Abu Ali's blue eyes burn with hatred.

We've hit a nerve. I press it harder.

"Look at all the violence going on. Your neighborhood has been ruined. Your life has been ruined. Is that what you want for your son?"

He mumbles something then sinks within himself again. He looks even smaller, even more emaciated than the day before. Hadir shrugs and says, "I did not understand what he said."

"Look, Abu Ali, we Americans made plenty of mistakes. We didn't realize that the Shia would form militias and take over neighborhoods. We didn't know they would assassinate Sunni."

His cold blue eyes spear me. At least I have his attention.

"But that doesn't mean we can't work together to fix it now."

Silence.

"Who else will help you? The Syrians? The Saudis? The Jordanians? None of them are going to come to your rescue."

More silence.

"We want to help."

"You caused this!" he barks.

Good, we've got him emotional. Now I'll hit him hard with a Love of Family approach.

"But you've got nobody else. Who else is going to help? Al Qaida?"

"Al Qaida cannot help us."

The words seem to slip out inadvertently, and Abu Ali looks surprised at the admission.

"What about the suicide bombings? Is that what you want for Iraq? More violence?"

He stammers. Hadir watches him intently. Abu Ali finally bursts out, "It was the only weapon we had." Hadir mirrors his vocal inflections. He sounds desperate to believe his own words.

Bobby jumps in and goes for the throat, "Abu Ali, do you want your son to grow up in this cycle of violence? Do you want him living in an Iraq where he can't even go to the market without getting blown up?"

Defiance flares in him. "I would be happy to see my son die. He would die a martyr."

Bobby and I both sense he doesn't mean it.

"Come on, Abu Ali. Your only son. You would give your only son to this insanity?"

"Yes."

"Bullshit!" Bobby yells. "That's fucking bullshit and you know it!"

46

Bobby is throwing his last ace. And then Abu Ali's head drops ever so slightly.

"I just want things back the way they were," he says in a gentle voice.

We've gotten to him.

"Your son doesn't have to die," Bobby says.

Abu Ali rubs at the water in his eyes. He struggles to maintain his composure and squirms in his chair.

"I want my son to live in peace."

"Well he won't. He'll live in this violence, in this hell, unless you do something about it."

A long silence fills the interrogation booth. We wait him out. The tears slow.

"There are two farmhouses south of Abu Ghraib in Yusufiyah."

Bobby leaps at this. "What are they used for?"

"They rotate through them. They are used for blessing suicide bombers."

"Will you show us where they are?"

Abu Ali looks at Bobby and then looks at me and then back at Bobby.

"Yes."

Bobby reaches for the laptop on the table between us. It's loaded with digital satellite maps of Iraq that display on the flat-screen TV on the wall. Bobby scrolls through the maps and follows the route from Baghdad onto the main western highway toward Abu Ghraib. Abu Ali recognizes a bridge on the highway and slowly he works his way south on the map and locates the first farmhouse. It's a lone house in the middle of farmland. The closest neighbor is a mile away. When we mark the location, Abu Ali says, "This place is sometimes used for meetings. Suicide bombers gather there as well."

"Meetings between whom?" Bobby asks.

"I don't know."

He's not willing to go that far yet.

Then Abu Ali asks Bobby to return the map to Abu Ghraib. From there he tracks north on a minor road and then down a dirt path to another farmhouse.

"That one," Abu Ali says.

"What's this one used for?" Bobby asks.

"Sometimes they store weapons there."

"Thank you Abu Ali. You have helped us and you have helped Iraq."

"I did not do it for you. I did it for my son."

"My friend," Bobby says, "tell us who you and Zaydan work for and we can help you get back to your son. You can get back to taking care of your family."

That's too much. Abu Ali shakes his head. His eyes go icy again.

"I cannot tell you that."

"Cannot or will not?" Bobby demands.

"I want my son to live."

"We can protect you and your family."

Silence. This time, it endures. We get nothing further from Abu Ali. He shuts down, resolved to his fate, and we send him back to his cell.

Afterwards, we huddle with Cliff back at the 'gator pit. We show the analyst the locations Abu Ali gave us of the safe houses. We mention that he said meetings are sometimes held at the first and weapons at the second.

"This one farmhouse looks familiar," Cliff says. He turns to Bobby.

"Isn't this the one that you got from a previous detainee? The police source?"

"I think so," Bobby replies.

"Well, this is good stuff, gentlemen," Cliff says with a smile. "We'll pass this on to the SF guys and see what they can find."

We return to our desks and get back to work. In a few hours, we're scheduled to interrogate Zaydan one final time before he goes to Abu Ghraib. If we don't get anything from him today, he'll take his secrets to the grave.

Five

THE CONVENIENT
CAR BOMB

THE NEXT MORNING I reach the 'gator pit by 10:30. I find doc Brady standing next to his desk looking thoroughly outraged over Bobby's latest prank. A piece-of-shit rinky-dink metal chair is handcuffed to his desk. This is Iraq and we work in a prison. Everyone carries handcuff keys. I try not to laugh at his predicament as I slide into my own chair, which is so beat up that nobody wants to monkey with it.

The whiteboard has a new Randyism for the day. It reads, "Jesus can walk on water, but Randy can swim through land."

The Doc goes off on his morning chair search. As soon as he disappears, Bobby arrives, Cliff in tow. Somebody flicks on the flat-screen TV at the front of the 'gator pit and tunes it to CNN and a breaking report from Yusufiyah. A suicide

50

car bomber just tried to run a checkpoint manned by marines. He detonated in a crowd, killing and wounding dozens of Iraqi civilians. There are no reports of marine deaths.

"Fucking Muj," Bobby says through clenched teeth.

Muj, like mooch with a "j," is short for mujahideen. Muj are the new Charlies.

"Foreign fighter, probably," Cliff notes.

"How do you know that?" I ask.

"Since I've been here, I have yet to see a single Iraqi suicide bomber. They're all foreign volunteers. Young males, eighteen to twenty-five. Some of the unsuccessful ones come through here."

As we're glued to CNN, Randy walks up to us. "Bobby, last day on Zaydan. He talks or walks."

"Fuckin' A."

"Shit-hot job yesterday. We put surveillance assets on those safe houses Abu Ali gave us. The first one was empty, but they'll keep checking it from time to time. The second one the guys are planning to hit tonight."

The live report from Yusufiyah grabs our attention again. Randy stands next to us, arms crossed, staring at the carnage. After a minute he swears lightly, then checks his watch. "Time for the morning meeting," he calls to us as he heads to the conference room.

We're assigned to interrogate Zaydan today, along with a couple of detainees low on the totem pole. Bobby decides the time is right for a Prisoner's Dilemma approach.

Early that afternoon, we sit down with Zaydan. Hadir serves as our 'terp again. Bobby starts by saying how much we want to help him, then, weaving in the Prisoner's Dilemma, mentions that Abu Ali has given us information.

Zaydan is cordial, but he doesn't buy it. He offers us nothing.

During a lull, Bobby tries to lighten the mood. "Hey Matthew," he asks, "Zaydan told me a great joke. Wanna hear it?"

Hadir translates this. Our big detainee chuckles.

"Sure," I play along.

Bobby turns to Zaydan and says, "Correct me if I get this wrong, okay?"

"Certainly."

Bobby starts in. "Did ya hear the one about the al Dulaimi who went to the soccer game?"

An al Dulaimi is a member of the largest tribe in Iraq. There are at least six million al Dulaimis in country.

"No, haven't heard that one."

Bobby grins and looks over at Zaydan, who wears a Cheshire-cat smile.

"Well, he goes home and runs into his cousin, right?"

Hadir translates. Zaydan nods.

"Okay, so he says to his cousin, he says 'Hey! I just got back from the soccer game, and boy was it exciting! Guess who won?' "

Zaydan can't contain himself. He starts giggling. He brings his hands up to his mouth to cover his laughter, and I notice he has chubby fingers.

"So the cousin shakes his head and says, 'I already know!' "

Both Bobby and Zaydan start howling. Even Hadir cracks up. I alone sit unmoved.

"What's the matter? Don't you get it? Hadir does and he's a Kurd," Bobby says.

"Yeah. I get it. The al Dulaimi are gossipers. News travels fast. That sort of thing, right?"

"Yeah. There's a lot of those al Dulaimi motherfuckers."

"I guess it's sort of an Iraqi inside joke." I make an effort to grin. Zaydan's still belly-laughing. He looks like an Arab jolly ol' St. Nick, only with an *I recruit killers for Al Qaida* sort of dark side.

"You can't throw a rock in Iraq and not hit an al Dulaimi," Hadir opines.

It takes a minute to restore decorum in the interrogation booth. Bobby sips some water. Zaydan plays with his chubby fingers. Hadir polishes off his second Coke of the session. I sit next to the lone desk in the room, pen in hand waiting for us to continue.

Finally, Bobby nukes the jovial atmosphere. "Zaydan, you are going to be leaving us soon. I wish I could help you, but you've got to give us something. Anything. Please, we like you."

Zaydan frowns and shakes his head curtly.

"I cannot give you what you want."

Bobby suddenly erupts. "Damn'it! I'm trying to save you! Help me help you!" He emphasizes the last words with a palm-slap to his notebook. Zaydan looks surprised. He sits up in his chair, his eyebrows arch, and he crosses his arms. Bobby stares at him. Zaydan says nothing. He averts his gaze.

"Fuckin' A, man! Give me something!"

"I can't."

Bobby lets out an exasperated "Fuck it!" and gets to his feet.

What's going on? Bobby, what are you doing?

Bobby hovers over our detainee and gazes at him. Zaydan freezes, unsure of what's happening.

Bobby pivots and walks out the door without another word. Hadir and I exchange quizzical glances. We're left in awkward silence.

What am I going do now? Should I leave and follow Bobby? No. Stay here. Engage Zaydan. Build rapport.

What do I say after this? I'm not sure. My mind races.

Start with the basics. Start on his turf.

"So, uh, Zaydan?"

"Yes?" Zaydan sounds rattled.

"How long have you been an imam?"

"For about fifteen years."

Keep going. He liked that question.

"Have you memorized the Koran?"

"Not all of it, but most."

"I'm reading the Koran now," I tell him. This piques his interest.

"Really?"

"Yes, I'm surprised to find that some of the stories in the Bible are also in the Koran."

"Yes, that's true, but they are a little different."

We start talking about the Angel Gabriel and how he came to Mary. According to Zaydan, the immaculate conception is made after Mary goes into the desert and drinks from a stream that appears at her feet to quench her thirst and then eats a fig from a tree.

I marvel at this. "Wow. That's different from what I learned in the Bible. But you know, it is amazing that you're a Muslim and I'm a Christian, yet we believe in the same story."

Actually, I'm not a Christian. I'm part humanist and part Buddhist. But in the booth, I become whatever and whoever can build rapport with the detainee.

"We are people of the same book," I say. "We're both believers."

Zaydan loves this discussion.

"Are you interested in learning more about Islam?" he asks.

Before I can answer the door slams open. Bobby storms inside, a portable phone to his ear. "Zaydan!" he starts, but he's out of breath. He gasps for air.

"Yes?" Zaydan's face is puzzled.

"There was a bomb, a bomb at the compound this morning."

The news stuns our detainee. "What?"

"The compound where your family lives! The one our marines are fucking guarding! A suicide car bomber rammed the damn checkpoint! There are bodies fucking everywhere! I just saw it on CNN."

It was Zaydan's compound that we saw. He'd said the marines guard it.

As Hadir translates the words in a raised voice, I realize I'm on the edge of my chair.

"Look, I've got the marine commander on the phone. I want him to send some soldiers to check on your family. What number is your apartment?"

Zaydan looks panicked. His eyes bulge. His face flushes bright crimson. "Uh, um . . ."

"Hurry up!" Bobby yells.

"My apartment number?"

"Yes. Hurry up! The colonel is waiting!"

Bobby's urgency prompts Zaydan to say, "Building five, number one hundred and four."

Bobby repeats it. Zaydan nods.

"Okay, sir, you there? I've got the address. It's building five, number one zero four. Did you get that?" Bobby ducks a bit and blocks his other ear.

"Sir, I can't hear you."

Zaydan looks apoplectic.

"Sir, you there?" Bobby mutters to himself. "Shit, I think I lost him."

Hadir translates that quietly. Zaydan emits a low moan, his hands come up to the sides of his head, and he mutters something to Allah.

"Yes, sir! That's right. Building five, one zero four! Right. Okay. Call us back when you know something. Thank you, sir." He lowers the phone slightly and says, "Zaydan, they're sending people to check right now."

The tension in the room is so thick that Bobby seems to swim through it as he paces back and forth.

"Zaydan. I pray everyone is safe." My words sound stilted.

Bobby blurts, "I'll be right back. I'm going to check on something." He vanishes through the doorway, leaving me, Hadir, and Zaydan to stare after him.

Zaydan crumbles under the weight of the unknown. His face falls into his beefy hands and he mumbles a prayer. His voice cracks. Is he crying? I can't tell. As the wait continues, he slaps his forehead repeatedly. This is an Arabic sign of extreme duress and angst.

Hadir and I share another glance. We're both wide-eyed

and stunned. I can't believe I didn't make the connection this morning. I wonder what triggered it for Bobby.

Zaydan rocks back and forth in his chair, still slapping himself, and mumbling.

"Allah," is all I can make out of his words.

The minutes pass. Were I in his shoes, I don't know how long I could take the suspense.

What can I say to this man?

I say nothing. I know Zaydan is picturing his wife amongst the dead and maimed; his girl, broken and bloodied by the debris thrown as shrapnel by the exploding car. Those are mental images no father, no husband ever hopes to endure, especially one who has played a role in this sort of carnage. Does he feel guilty?

Bobby returns ten minutes later. He appears in the door and presses the phone to his ear. "What Sir! I'm still here. What's that? Say again?"

Zaydan stops rocking. Now he's as still as a corpse, focused on Bobby. In seconds he goes from cherubic to ghostly.

Bobby clicks off the phone and pockets it. He pins his eyes on Zaydan.

"Is my family alive?" he pleads.

Hadir struggles to repeat the words, but finally he says, "He wants to know if his family is alive."

"Yes. Your wife answered the door," Bobby replies. Zaydan's shoulders sag. Relief washes over him.

"Your wife said everyone is okay. The bomb did not hurt your family. They were inside the apartment when it exploded. They're scared, but okay."

"Allah be praised! Allah be praised!" Zaydan bursts out.

Bobby sits down in front of Zaydan, "They're okay my friend."

"Thank you. Thank you for doing this for me, my friend."

"No problem. We're here to do whatever we can for you."

Zaydan isn't finished. He grows effusive, "I am so thankful for what you have done. Bless you."

"Zaydan, there are a lot of dead Sunnis at the checkpoint. They are your neighbors. The marines who protect your family—some of them are also dead."

"God's will."

"No," Bobby lowers his voice and softens it. "Next time it could be your wife or your daughter. Help us end this violence. Give us something."

Zaydan lets out a long sigh.

"We're not here to harm Iraqis," Bobby continues. "You know that. We want to find the foreigners who have come here and caused all this violence."

Zaydan doesn't react, but I can tell he's hanging on Bobby's words.

"Look, Abu Ali told us about a farmhouse. One used by suicide bombers."

"Show me the house." Zaydan says.

Maybe he's going to play.

Bobby turns to the laptop and brings up the satellite maps on the flat-screen TV. He walks Zaydan down the highway from Baghdad to Abu Ghraib and then over the bridge and south into Yusufiyah, but stops short of the farmhouse that Abu Ali gave us.

"Keep going south," Zaydan says.

Bobby scrolls the map to the south. We all watch the thin trail of orange dirt below the cursor as the map continues to move.

"There," Zaydan says. "That house next to the road."

It is the same one Abu Ali noted. Either that place is significant, or they've all been told to give that house up should they be captured.

"What is this house?" Bobby asks.

"They have meetings there," Zaydan says.

Bobby decides to press. "Zaydan, this is extremely helpful. Thank you."

"I am grateful to you, my friend. My family is everything."

"Then help us keep them safe. Give us the name of your boss."

Zaydan shakes his head firmly. "I cannot. If I were to do that . . ." He falters.

Hadir waits for him to finish. When he doesn't, he shrugs at Bobby.

"Zaydan? We've offered you an olive branch of friendship here."

"I know. I cannot tell you more."

I don't think he's loyal to Al Qaida. He's afraid of whomever he works for, and we won't be able to quell that fear.

Bobby senses this, too. "Okay, Zaydan. Just know that we'll always reach out to you, buddy, no matter what you do."

"Thank you, my friend, thank you."

We end the interrogation. Zaydan goes back to his holding cell. He'll be transferred to Abu Ghraib tonight. He'll eventually be tried in court and, because of his role in aiding suicide bombings, he'll get the death sentence and hang. If he's really lucky, he'll only get life in one of Iraq's Shia-run prisons, which is the same as death.

As Bobby and I walk back to the 'gator pit, I ask, "That's amazing that you realized the bomber hit Zaydan's compound."

"Yeah, it struck me after I left."

"How'd you get the marine commander on the phone so quickly?"

Bobby stops in mid-stride. He turns to me with a wicked half-smile and says, "I didn't."

I'm confused. "What do you mean?"

"There was no one on the other end of the line. Fucking phone doesn't even work."

Love is the ultimate weapon.

Six

THE BURNING HOUSE

H EY, MATTHEW," CLIFF says to me as I arrive the
following morning.
"What's up, Cliff?"
"Check out this video. We just got it from the SF guys."

I walk over to Cliff's desktop. Bobby's already there. Cliff
explains, "This was taken by one of the SF teams. They were
hitting one of the safe houses Abu Ali gave up, right? Well, as
they approached, they started taking fire."

"What did they do?" I ask.

"Watch."

Cliff starts the video. It shows a white, flat-roofed house
with a white sedan parked nearby. It appears to be a tranquil
daylight scene taken by someone on the ground less than a
hundred yards from the house.

After twenty seconds of this, Bobby gets impatient.
"Boring Cliff. Come on."

Suddenly, the house disintegrates. Pieces of masonry fly in all directions. Smoke billows out and up, swallowing the white car. Secondary explosions follow, throwing more smoke and debris into the air. When it clears, the house is gone. Only a heap of burning rubble remains.

"Boring, eh?" Cliff says snidely. "The SF guys called in an air strike. Didn't want to risk entering the house with possible suicide bombers inside." He pulls out a bottle of nasal spray and uses it. "Sorry." Like all new arrivals to our piece of Iraq, he's contracted a sinus infection.

Bobby has an idea. "You know, Matthew, we can use this with Abu Ali."

"What do you mean, like a Love of Comrade approach?"

"Yeah. What do you think?"

I shake my head. "I don't think it'll work. Very risky."

Bobby shrugs. "He's not talking now and he's on his way out. Let's just throw the dice and see if this opens him up."

David, our senior interrogator, joins our group. "Matthew," he says to me, "Why don't you join me this afternoon in the monitor room to watch the other interrogations. You'll be doing that a lot in the weeks ahead, so you might as well get used to it."

I look at Bobby.

"Go ahead," he says. "You can watch my handsome mug from that Hollywood room."

"You sure?" I ask.

"Damn sure," Bobby says.

"Come on, I'll show you how to work the controls," David says.

I look Bobby over before I follow David. Bobby looks exhausted. His eyes have dark circles and his shoulders are

slightly slumped. All week we've stayed long after our shifts
have ended to write our reports. Bobby's a stickler for details
and always triple-checks to make sure the reports are in the
proper format. I haven't gotten back to my hooch before
3 A.M. all week.

"Hey, have you gotten any sleep?" I ask. He picks up a
Coke can and raises it as if he's going to offer a toast. "Forty-
eight hours straight!"

David leads me into the Hollywood room and explains
how it works. On one wall are three rows of state-of-the-art
flat-screen TVs. Below the flat-screens is a long desk with
several electronic switchboxes that control the cameras and
audio in each of the booths. On the back wall are four cus-
tomized roof-high glass cases with stacks of electronic com-
ponents. The whole room is a hack-job of wires and buttons,
and it nearly requires a masters degree to operate. Big Brother
is watching. It's a great way for the senior 'gator to keep tabs
on what techniques the other 'gators are using.

"Have a seat," David offers. As elsewhere, the chairs here
are worn and broken.

Bobby appears on one of the flat-screen displays. Abu Ali
follows a few minutes later. I grab a set of headphones, flip a
switch, and tune in. As I watch, I'm really taken by Bobby's
physical appearance. The vibrant Nebraskan I've gotten to
know this week is gone. Instead, I see a young man who has
pushed himself too far, worked too hard. It is a lesson we all
learn. Back when I was a shiny 2nd Lieutenant, I didn't know
how to pace myself either. Now, in my mid-thirties, I've
learned that this sort of deployment is not a sprint; it's a mar-
athon. You've got to apportion your energy for the entire
race; otherwise you'll crash and burn early.

Bobby's on the brink. As he starts working with Abu Ali, he sounds testy and impatient.

"Abu Ali, we need to know who you work for," Bobby begins.

Our detainee doesn't answer. Bobby repeats the question only to get the same result.

"I thought you agreed to work with us?" Bobby asks angrily.

Abu Ali replies, "You Americans have lied from the beginning."

He's retrenched, retreated back into his shell of bitterness. Coaxing him out at this point is going to be tough, if not impossible.

Bobby works hard to get him talking, but Abu Ali barely responds to his questions. In some cases, he doesn't answer at all.

"Abu Ali, help us save lives. You said you'd join us."

Silence.

"We're trying to help you."

No response.

Bobby slams his hand down on his notebook and in a fit of frustration shouts, "Is that all you're going to do? Fuckin' sit there? You're not going to say anything? How's that going to help Iraq? How's that going to help your *son*?"

"I gave you the houses."

"Yes, and I thought that you would join us."

"I can't."

Bobby looks ready to blow his stack. Instead, he says, "You know what, Abu Ali? I'm gonna show you a video."

Abu Ali has been staring at the floor through most of this. Now he glances up. I see he's curious.

"Yeah. That's right. It'll show you what the future of Iraq holds if we can't work together."

Bobby flips open his laptop and places it on the single table in the room. He puts in a CD, and the image appears on the large flat-screen TV on the wall in front of them.

"Watch this," Bobby says. He presses a button, and the video rolls.

My camera is looking from above the flat-screen TV down at Abu Ali's face. For the first twenty seconds, his face is a mask. It shows no emotion at all. Suddenly, he bends over double, as if someone has just kicked him in the stomach. He's facing the floor, and I can see spatters on the concrete. Tears. He's sobbing.

Bobby shuts the video off, closes the laptop, and says, "That's what happens to people who support suicide bombers." He turns and sees Abu Ali's condition. "What's the matter?"

Abu Ali says nothing. He sobs silently. After a minute, he sits back up in his chair. His cheeks are slick with tears; his eyes are haunted and full of loathing. Gone is the mask. The transformation startles Bobby.

"Abu Ali? What is it?"

No response. The two sit in silence. The tears keep pouring down Abu Ali's face. A minute passes. Then two. I notice Abu Ali isn't looking at Bobby at all anymore. He sets his gaze on the floor and doesn't budge it.

"Abu Ali, talk to me," Bobby says.

Finally, in a broken voice, Abu Ali says, "That was my friend's house."

I feel a stab of compassion for him. Bobby seems to as well. We made him watch his own friend's death—one that he orchestrated by giving us the safe house's location in the first place.

Bobby tries to rally. "Abu Ali, you don't know that your friend was there."

"He was there."

"How can you know that?"

"He owns the white car. When it is parked there, he is home."

He bends over again, clutching his hands to his face. A despairing moan escapes him.

Bobby plays his last card. "This doesn't have to happen, Abu Ali. If you tell us who you work for and who else is in your network, we can go and pick them up like we did with you and Zaydan. They won't have to die like this. You can save the rest of them. Work with me."

Abu Ali sits up straight and wipes the final tears from his eyes.

"Never."

It is futile. I can see by Abu Ali's expression that he's done. Bobby senses it, too, and pleads with him. Abu Ali won't even look at him. He doesn't utter another word.

I pull off the headphones and head for the 'gator pit. My stomach churns. We should not have done this to Abu Ali, but Bobby didn't know the significance of the video. Abu Ali is doomed, and now, in the days before he hangs, he will live with the knowledge that he betrayed his friend.

I have to remind myself that he is the enemy. He blessed suicide bombers, men who kill women and children in crowded markets in order to further engulf Iraq in this chaos and violence. Yet I cannot help but feel sorry for him. His life is over, ruined by the decisions he's made ever since the

Badr Corps came knocking at his door. And although I don't sympathize with his tactics, I can understand his desire to defend himself and his family.

Bobby and I meet by our desks.

"Oh my God," he says as he sees me. "Did you see that?"

"Yeah. Sometimes when you roll the dice, you lose big."

"I feel like shit."

"No, don't worry about it. Who would have thought he would give up a house that his friend still lived in?"

Bobby agrees with me, but I see in his face that he's hit the wall.

"You need to get some sleep."

He nods absently. "He shut down. He won't give anyone anything else."

"Well," I say, "at least we still have the other house."

PART II

COMING INTO FOCUS

Limitations on the use of methods identified herein as expressly prohibited should not be confused with psychological ploys, verbal trickery, or other nonviolent or noncoercive ruses used by the interrogator in the successful interrogation of hesitant or uncooperative sources.

—ARMY MANUAL FIELD MANUAL 34–52,
INTELLIGENCE INTERROGATION

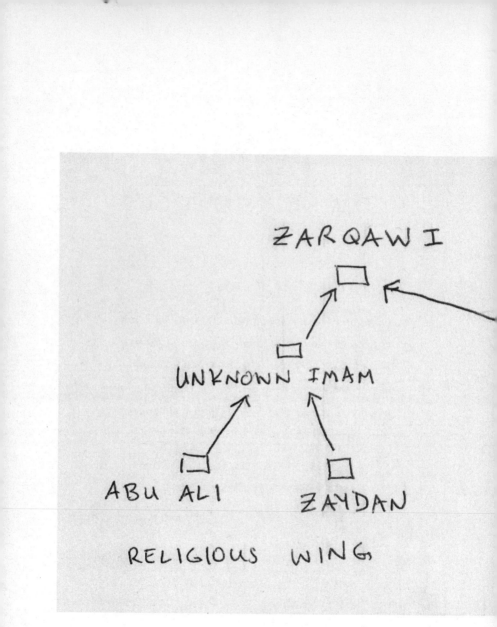

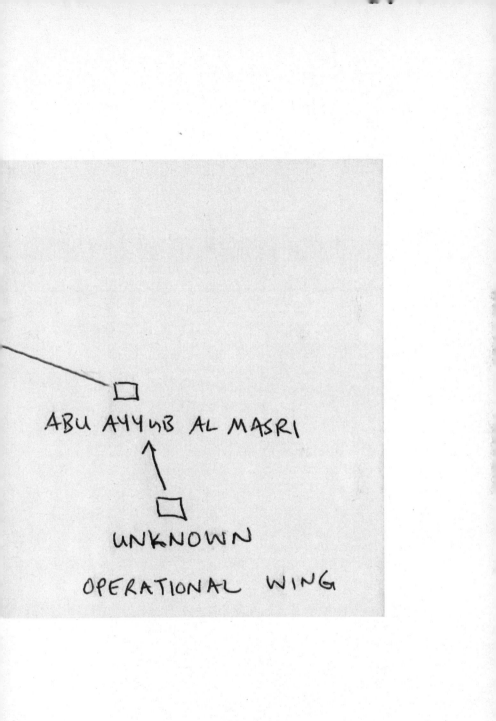

ABU AYYUB AL MASRI

UNKNOWN

OPERATIONAL WING

Seven

FRACTURES

EARLY APRIL, 2006

F OR THE PAST two weeks we've spun our wheels. What little intel we've gleaned from the detainees has yielded nothing that brings us closer to Zarqawi. The pressure mounts in tandem with the chaos on the street. Zarqawi's momentum is growing as the suicide bombings increase, as well as the retaliatory attacks, and all-out civil war seems imminent. ███████████████████████ ████████████████████████████████████ ███████████████████████ We need to find a way to climb Al Qaida's chain of command.

There's more at play amongst the 'gators than the need to get the job done. ███████████████████████ ██████████████████ I've sat with David in the Hollywood room, monitoring interrogations. It doesn't take long to discover we have a deep division amongst us. There is the old guard, who were at Guantánamo and did previous tours in Afghanistan and Iraq. They believe in the fear-and-control

73

methods but now they're being forced to play by the rules. Then there is my group and a few other 'gators who are starting to embrace our new methods.

One morning, I arrive at the 'gator pit early. The night-shift 'gators are still busy typing up their reports, and most of the desks are still occupied. ███████████████

███████████████████████████████████

███████████████████████████████████

███████████████████████████

I spot Ann pecking away at a keyboard. I sit down next to her. She looks up from her flat-screen monitor and smiles.

"How'd it go last night?" I ask.

"Frustrating. I've got this operations guy I know has to be important, but I can't get through to him. He's done a lot of really bad things, and he's resigned to his fate."

"Inshallah."

"Yeah. Exactly."

"Have you shown him any sympathy?"

Ann shakes her head, "Not really. What do you have in mind?"

Lenny, a night-shift 'gator from New York City, overhears this and guffaws. "Fucking muj. Just show him who's boss."

I turn to look at him. Lenny's an old-schooler, a veteran 'gator who got pulled out of Guantánamo and sent here, a fate that has left him thoroughly pissed off. ███████████

███████████████████████████████████

███████████████████████████████████

██████████

"What do you mean?" I ask him. Ann doesn't look at him, just sets her jaw and looks grim.

"Well look, these muj won't give you nothin' unless you

take charge. Take the muj I've got right now. He'll come around, believe me. Once he gets it through his thick skull that he's going to hang."

I'm annoyed. One thing we were taught back at Fort Huachuca was never to use derogatory terms to describe our detainees. Dehumanizing them is the first step down the slippery slope to torture. It also exposes Lenny's ignorance; not all of the detainees here are true mujahideen.

I decide to ignore him. I turn back to Ann. "Your detainee is a Sunni, right?"

"Aren't they all?"

"Yeah. And most of them have been terrorized by Shia militias like the Badr Corps and Mahdi Army. At least most of the ones I've met so far have been. If you show sympathy towards him because of this, maybe he'll open up."

Lenny guffaws again. "Sympathy won't work. Control 101 is the first lesson in interrogation. They're the enemy for Christ's sake."

I go to my desk to retrieve a binder. I hand it to Ann. "Look, I've put together some information about the Shia militias. It may be worth a shot."

Ann takes the binder and thanks me. Lenny looks disgusted. I hear him mutter, "Sympathy for a haji. Right."

The old ways die hard.

Later that morning, David asks me to sit with him in the Hollywood room and observe the afternoon's interrogations. Steve and Tom are slated to question a detainee we think is the highest-level Al Qaida operative in our system. Steve's a devotee of the new techniques, one of our group who went through training at Fort Huachuca with me. Tom is a father of four with a gray beard who gives the impression that he is a decade older than his thirty six years. Tom is old-school. He understands control and dominance but in the past has seemed more open to the new ideas than some of the other veteran 'gators.

This should be an interesting match. I put on a set of headphones and tune in as the detainee enters the interrogation booth. The prisoner, like Zaydan, is an imam who preaches at a Baghdad mosque. He's fat and sloppy with wide eyes and a bushy gray beard. He looks like he's led the good life while convincing others to die in suicide attacks.

Steve starts off with him by establishing rapport. They discuss the imam's mosque, his background, and his family. It seems routine enough at first. Then Tom orders the imam to his feet. He puts the detainee against a wall. Steve approaches and stands right next to him. Tom stands face-to-face with him. For a moment I get anxious. Is this going to get out of hand?

Both 'gators suddenly launch a barrage of questions at him. They pummel him with rapid-fire, unconnected questions that force his mind to jump from one place to another in a split second.

"Who do you work for?"

"What's your wife's name again?"

"Do you want me to help you?"

"Where do you live?"

"What mosque do you preach at?"

"Who do you work for?"

"How many sons do you have?"

"Do you want to be my friend?"

"Where did you meet besides the mosque?"

The imam goes from confident and slightly smug to desperately confused. He tries to answer the questions as they come, but he can't keep up. He stumbles over his answers, mixes things up, and grows even more anxious and uneasy. His voice kicks up an octave as he tries to respond. Tom and Steve have pushed him well outside his comfort zone.

As the staccato questions continue, he starts tripping over his lies. This approach can be very effective. My group has been trained to search out what motivates a detainee, then use that motivation to our advantage. That takes time, rapport, and a measure of trust between 'gator and detainee. The approach Tom and Steve are using works in a different way. Instead of using a ruse, the direct questioning at this pace prevents the detainee from thinking through his lies. As they go over the same territory again and again, discrepancies start to appear.

The imam begins to crumble. Steve and Tom home in on those areas where he trips up, battering away at him with more questions. By the end of the interrogation, the imam reveals that his mosque recruited for Al Qaida. He gives up the location of several more safe houses where suicide bombers meet and prepare for their missions. He also tells them that he raised money for Al Qaida. It's no secret that the religious wing of Al Qaida Iraq plays a major role in funding the insurgency.

By the end of the interrogation, both David and I are impressed by the way Steve and Tom work together. They blend the old-school techniques and the new ones to powerful effect. Though they don't get the imam to give up his boss, they do get a lot of useful information out of him.

Next we watch an interrogation that Mary's running by herself. The difference is stark. She sits down with her detainee but makes no attempt to build rapport with him. Instead, she shows signs of contempt for the prisoner and uses control techniques to demonstrate that she's in charge. Then she rattles off the questions her partnered analyst wants answers to, but the detainee reveals nothing. When she finishes the list, she ends the interrogation. I'm puzzled; I can't figure out what she's doing. One thing is clear, though, she has never been exposed to the new techniques.

Late that afternoon, Bobby conducts a solo interrogation. He's clearly one of us. He throws all sorts of curveballs at his detainee, running multiple approaches mixed every now and then with a clever ruse. Seeing him work impresses me all over again. If he can learn to pace himself, he'll be one of the best 'gators in the business.

Before I leave that night, Randy takes me aside. "Listen, we're still watching the safe house outside Abu Ghraib that Abu Ali and Zaydan gave up. That was good stuff you got."

"Thanks."

"If you get results, you'll change minds around here. Do you understand?"

"Yes."

"You don't have much time."

When I get back to my hooch some time after three in the morning, I fall asleep repeating those words.

I get back to the 'gator pit at about 10 A.M., an hour before the night shift ends. Once again, I find Ann typing away at her computer. Lenny sits a few tables away, cursing at something.

"Hey, thanks for that suggestion," Ann says to me. "He opened up a little bit. It got him talking. Before, I couldn't get a thing out of him."

"A little sympathy goes a long way."

Lenny overhears this and grumbles, "I don't see why you waste your time with that stuff."

Ann doesn't rise to the bait. Neither do I.

There's an awkward silence until Bobby bounds up to me.

"Hey, you gotta check something out," he says.

"What?"

"The SF guys captured this ▮▮▮ last night. Unbelievable."

I follow Bobby to his computer. For a moment, the screen is blank. Then the video opens with a bound man on his knees in a dirt field. Two Sunni insurgents stand on either side of him behind black masks. Their prisoner, who can't be more than twenty-four, looks like an academic. He wears glasses, is clean shaven, and is distressingly calm. As I watch, I want to scream at him to run. Something very bad is about to happen.

One of the insurgents steps to the camera. He utters a few words as he unsheathes a long, wicked-looking knife. Behind him, the prisoner still appears calm, as if this, too, is God's will.

The knife-wielding insurgent steps away from the camera, goes behind the prisoner, and pushes him forward. With his arms bound, the academic falls face-first into the dirt. The insurgent reaches down, grabs a mass of his hair, then jerks it upward. His head flies up out of the dirt, and now he's suspended by his hair, neck stretched, dull eyes on the cameraman. He's still calm, but now I see fear in his eyes.

The insurgent cuts his throat from ear to ear. Blood spurts

from his severed arteries in quick pulses. The dirt before him turns crimson. He'll bleed out and die on camera. I pray that it is quick.

But the insurgent isn't done. He brings the knife down again, but this time, instead of slashing, he hacks. The dying man gurgles and coughs. The insurgent saws away at the neck. Blood pours. It is a ghastly sight.

The academic's head flops and lolls. His body spasms. His fingers and arms twitch. The insurgent starts hacking harder, and I see bone through the gore. The insurgent, unable to sever his victim's head, grows frustrated. He slashes, then tugs again, and the head tears partly away from the ruined neck. Still, he can't get it free.

The second insurgent walks over and takes the knife. He swings the blade down and with a few strokes precise to the neck, he cuts the head free. The body lies twitching in a growing pool of blood as he holds up his trophy. The cameraman zooms in on the second insurgent's face. His eyes show through the peepholes of his black hood. They are triumphant.

The file ends.

"Goddamn," Bobby says in a voice full of vitriol.

I have no words for it.

I am not a stranger to gore and horror. Back in the States, one of my first cases as a criminal investigator turned out to be about as awful as they come. Two airmen accidentally hit and killed a bicyclist near my base in Tucson. The cyclist's head went through the windshield and landed on the seat between the two airmen. When I arrived on the scene, one of the airmen had fled, crying "My life is over." We tracked the runaway airman back to his apartment, where we discovered he'd swallowed a shotgun barrel and pulled the trigger. We found bits of his skull in adjoining rooms . . . and his intact brain in the bathtub.

"Matthew?"

Bobby's looking at me with earnest concern.

"I'm all right," I say.

My mind is replaying the scene we've just watched.

"Good. There's one more, and you ain't seen nothing yet."

I'm rooted in place. Bobby clicks on another file. The media player reveals another macabre scene. This time, the camera pans down along a line of about thirty prisoners, bound with their hands behind their backs. They're all men and boys, ranging in age from teens to senior citizens. All of them look utterly despondent. They sit quietly, resigned to their fate. Behind them, four insurgents pace back and forth. They're Sunni. One of them produces a pistol.

I want to yell at the prisoners to run.

None of the prisoners moves. The pistol cracks. A prisoner falls over, blood gushing from the exit wound in his forehead. The insurgent steps to another prisoner and pulls the trigger. He is slow, deliberate, ritualistic. A side step, the pistol comes down until the barrel hovers inches from the back of the next victim's head. He gives each one a few seconds of sheer terror as they wait for the bullet to end their lives. Then the pistol bucks, the report reaches the camera's microphone. The prisoner flops into the dirt.

The insurgent runs out of bullets. Still the remaining prisoners don't move. Another insurgent hands him a second pistol. He uses it to finish the job. By the time he reaches the last prisoner, the field is heaped with bleeding corpses.

The file ends and Bobby whispers, "Un-fucking-believable. How can you help but hate these people?"

I have no answer to that.

"Ever seen anything like that?"

"Never," I manage.

In my air force career, I've been to almost every continent and seen my share of trauma and tragedy. In South America, during a medical deployment, I watched a desperate mother bring a child to our doctors for treatment. I saw the child, bundled in blankets, laboring to breathe. She was only a few months old, and somehow she'd contracted a flesh-eating bacteria. It was too late to treat it. There was nothing we could do. I had to tell the mother that her child was going to die. I'll never forget watching her leave, sobbing as she carried her dying child on her chest.

Those are things that never leave a man. I have tried to live a life of balance, relying on logic and intelligence when confronted with overwhelming emotion. It is how I got by as a criminal investigator, especially when I had an abuse case involving children. But nothing in my career has prepared me for these two scenes Bobby has shared with me.

Treat them with sympathy.

He hacked the helpless academic's head off with a knife.

Treat them with respect and be sensitive to their cultural traditions.

Thirty men and boys lie executed in a field somewhere.

How can I do this job and not be consumed with hate? I don't want to become Lenny. I don't want to dehumanize my enemy. Yet what I just watched seems like pure evil.

I've never seen the world in terms of good and evil. To me that smacks of a religious overtone, a judgment call that we should not be making. Instead, I see the world in terms of tolerance. Ignorance versus knowledge. Fear versus understanding. These two videos are displays of hatred so fierce that it drives men to depravity. It is the hatred that I hate.

If I don't make a conscious choice about how to respond, my emotions will take over.

Pure hate. Pure malice. Torture and cruelty are their tools. To fight them, should I resort to hate? To bitterness and jaded contempt? Is that what it means to be a veteran 'gator around here?

I won't go down that path. There is no way it can exist alongside a yearning for peace and compassion. Intolerance must be rooted out if Iraq is to have a chance. Either way you look at it, the new ways work better. Hate and contempt don't get our prisoners talking. Yet after what I've seen today, I realize that it will take an Oscar-caliber performance in the interrogation booth to display the necessary respect and sympathy for my enemy.

Eight

THE OTHER SIDE OF
THE HOUSE

APRIL 10, 2006

T HE BLACK HELICOPTERS speed low across the ancient, checkerboard landscape of Yusufiyah. Stretching to the horizon is land that saw the evolution from nomad to city dweller at the heart of our efforts toward civilization. And for some five thousand years, since the rise of Sumer, Babylon, and the great Assyrian kings, it has been a dark heart riddled with violence and anguish.

Whump-whump-whump, helicopter rotor blades pound out a drumbeat that resonates across the countryside like a tribal warning.

The Americans are coming.

The helicopters streak toward their target. ███████████
██
██ The soldiers sit just above each skid, legs dangling in the wind, with only a D-ring and a belt to keep them from free-falling onto some Iraqi's farm. While such a method of travel would scare most civilians into a catatonic state, these men are veterans. They hold their weapons steady, even as their bodies are buffeted by the hundred-mile-an-hour slipstream.

The target, the farmhouse that Abu Ali gave up and Zaydan confirmed, swings into sight. For weeks, our part-time surveillance has uncovered nothing. But today, our asset spotted a blue truck and a white sedan parked out front. The soldiers launched within minutes.

The helicopters alight in precise positions around the farmhouse. The Special Forces spring into action, charging across open ground for the house.

Two men wearing bulky black vests try to escape from a back door. When the soldiers move to intercept them, they realize these men are human bombs. The vests bristle with explosives. The Americans have closed the gap; it is too late for the bombers to back off. The lead human bomb intuits this and with a sudden rush sprints toward the nearest American soldier, hoping to kill as many Americans as possible as he ignites. He doesn't get that chance. An M4 carbine barks. The suicide bomber spins violently, a bullet hole in his forehead. He manages to detonate himself as he falls, but the blast is focused into the ground and away from the soldiers who stand just ten meters away. The bomber's body is torn in half. Part of him lands in a ditch, his head scooped out, his eyes wide and horrified. Nobody who lives through such an attack can forget the sight of what C-4 explosive does to human flesh. It slices torsos, dismembers limbs, and extracts organs.

The other bomber goes down with another head shot before he can blow himself up. The two external threats are neutralized. Now the strike team must force its way into the house.

Every room must be cleared. Even the most benign farmhouse can become a death trap for American soldiers. Is there another bomber in the house? Are there insurgents lying in ambush, AK rifles shouldered, fingers on the triggers? Clearing a house is one of the most dangerous tasks a soldier can perform in Iraq. Al Qaida operatives sometimes wire their own safe houses with explosives. The entire house could be one big IED, ready to kill anyone who sets foot inside. It takes unique courage to go through a door not knowing what waits on the other side.

The entry team hits the front door, using violence and speed to overwhelm anyone who might resist, and catches a trio of suicide bombers in the front room. They hesitate; the Americans do not.

Shots ring out. Three more suicide bombers die before they can detonate.

The soldiers work from room to room in the one-story house, covering the hallways as they move. A swift kick on a door, and they push into a room, M4s at the ready. The first room is empty. The men move down the hall and kick in the door to the next room. Also empty. One more to go. They stack up and inch to the door. A gentle rock backward tells the other soldiers that the lead man is ready. The others push forward in response: everyone's ready to go. They kick in the door and pour inside.

This room is not empty. Not by a long shot.

Nine

THE GROUP OF FIVE

APRIL 10, 2006

W E HAVE SOMETHING significant today," announces Captain Randy as he plants a boot on his chair. The whole interrogation team is here, gathered for the 11 A.M. meeting in the conference room just off the 'gator pit.

"Earlier this morning, one of the teams caught five Iraqi males in a farmhouse. The team also killed five foreign suicide bombers in the raid." Randy pauses for effect. Even on the slowest days he can get our attention. We've been in country for only a few weeks, but his relentless energy has set a brisk pace for our unit. He is seemingly immune to exhaustion, and behind his back we've debated if he's even human. But this morning he doesn't need tricks to get our attention.

"The guys we picked up are well dressed and well educated. These are not your typical lowlifes building bombs in their basement. As of now, they are our top priority."

Randy pauses, then continues, "It's time to turn it up a notch. You've all heard what the colonel keeps telling us. These guys could be very close to Zarqawi. Let's get after them!"

Randy throws in a few expletives for effect, and the meeting breaks up.

We rush to the 'gator pit. Bobby and I are teamed with Cliff again. He comes over, leans on my desk as he wipes his nose, and says, "Care for some photos?" He hands a file folder to me, and I extract one. It is beyond horrible. The suicide bomber blew himself in half. His entrails blend with the earth below his torso. His face is pale and his black beard, thin and sharp, forms an outline around his face.

"We need to get these guys identified, if possible."

"What about evidence?" I ask Cliff while flipping through more photos of head shots.

"Not much. There was a video camera. Probably for filming last rites. There is a map of Baghdad that leads us to believe the targets were in Baghdad, but nothing definite."

"Okay, so what are the prisoners saying so far?"

"All of them say they'd gone to the house to attend a wedding."

"A wedding?" I ask, surprised. "Where was the bride?"

"Yeah, that's what I said. There was no bride." Cliff pushes his John Lennon glasses back up his nose, then hands me a few more documents. I see that I've been assigned to a prisoner named Abu Gamal, who is in his early sixties. A white sedan and a blue truck had been parked in front of the farmhouse, and Abu Gamal had the keys to the sedan in his pocket.

I look up at the whiteboard where the day's assignments

are written in blue ink. One of the other members of the Group of Five has been assigned to Nathan and Steve, and two members to Tom. The last member has been removed from the interrogations schedule by the doc for medical reasons.

"What else do we know about Abu Gamal?" I ask Cliff.

"Well, he was caught in the same room with the other four. They were all huddled in a circle. We have no idea where these guys fit into the network—or even what network, for that matter."

Cliff pauses to blow his nose again. He tosses a tissue toward a wastebasket and misses.

"Sorry I can't provide more background info."

"Don't worry," I say and smile at Bobby. "We'll work some magic."

"Look, we're starting from scratch here. Here's what we need to know."

I take notes as Cliff lays out the objectives for the day's interrogation. "What group do they work for? Why were they at the house? Who's in charge? Most important, though, we need to figure out where these guys fit in the chain of command. That's the top priority for now."

As Bobby runs to the refrigerator for the first of the day's four Cokes, I ease into my chair. It groans in protest but holds firm. Its black plastic legs and wheels have been abused so badly that it rolls like a broken grocery cart.

I throw the one-page summary of yesterday's raid onto the desk and study it again, searching for inspiration. Then I look back over the biographical sheet. Strategy is the key to any interrogation and to discovering a detainee's motivations. If I've identified what he wants, I can craft an incentive.

Bobby has watched me treat every detainee with civility and respect, and I do it because it is the right thing to do. But I also do it to establish rapport. The detainee and I will maneuver for position behind the mask of civility. Embedded in the initial small talk are loaded questions designed to unveil the unique passions that motivate or inspire him.

But we know nothing of Abu Gamal—he's a blank slate. I'll use basic questioning and approaches at first to see how he reacts to them. I go through a mental list of the approved approaches I might try in the first session. *Love of Family. Futility. Logical Reasoning. Fear Down. And rapport, always rapport. I'll start with that.*

The best interrogators are outstanding actors. Once they hit that booth, their personalities are transformed. They can tuck their reactions and biases into some remote corner of their minds and allow a doppelgänger to emerge. What doppelgänger is most likely to elicit information from a detainee changes from prisoner to prisoner. Sometimes I must have a wife or children so I can swap stories with the prisoner, though I have neither. Who I will be for Abu Gamal is still unknown. The doppelgänger will take its cue from every scrap of information Abu Gamal gives me about his motivations.

Bobby comes over to my desk, a Coke in hand. We talk strategy for a couple of minutes, and then it is time to meet Abu Gamal.

• • •

THE INTERROGATION BOOTH is kept intentionally sparse. It's furnished with four plastic lawn chairs, the type found in any suburban backyard. The prisoners sit against a plywood wall. Our interpreter sits in a corner adjacent to the prisoner. Before Abu Gamal arrives, I place my chair only a few feet from where his is positioned. Bobby will sit slightly behind me, a white plastic table to his right so he can jot down notes.

A guard opens the door, and Abu Gamal enters in handcuffs. A black mask covers his head.

"How do you want him?" the guard asks.

████████████████████████████████████

████████████████████████ The guard gives me a nod and uncuffs him. Abu Gamal rubs his wrists slightly as the cuffs come off. The guard helps him into his chair, then leaves. I hear the door shut behind me. We're almost ready to begin.

I order Abu Gamal to take off his mask. He pulls it off, giving me my first look at him.

He reminds me of an aged mole. A wizened face with a long, rodent-like nose and small, dark eyes set back into a squarish face. His beard is patchy, a scruffy salt-and-pepper mix that has grown unevenly across his jawline and almost to his eyes. His eyebrows are arched upward as if he is already entreating our mercy. He looks nervous and he's fiddling with his hands.

The interrogation begins.

We sit only a few feet apart, our legs almost touching. There's nothing between the two of us, no table as buffer to give him a comfort zone. It is my symbolic way of letting him know that I respect him and I'm not afraid to get personal. Some 'gators don't like to get this close to the prisoners. When I was in training at Fort Huachuca, rumors circulated that an interrogator once caught tuberculosis from a detainee. I thought it was nothing more than a soldierly urban legend, no reason to forfeit the advantages of body language and presence that can advance an interrogation. It is vital to make sure there are no barriers between the 'gator and the prisoner.

What motivates you, Abu Gamal? What do you care about most?

"Peace be with you," I say to him in Arabic.

He nods his head in return and replies, "Peace be upon you."

"*Schlonik?*" This is Iraqi slang for *How are you?*

Abu Gamal leans forward. He seems curiously eager. "I–I–I'm well, th–th–ank you."

Is the stuttering nerves? Or is it a speech impediment?

I glance at Hadir, our interpreter. He's ready. I switch to English, but I lock eyes with Abu Gamal. He needs to know the conversation is between us, despite the fact that it will flow through the 'terp. His eyes are very alert. He seems too ready, almost rehearsed.

"My name is Matthew and my coworker here is Bob. We look forward to working with you. I'm happy to have this opportunity to talk. How are you feeling?"

"I–I am f–f–f–fine." The stuttering strikes me as an act.

"Are you thirsty?" I point to a liter of bottled water sitting nearby. The Geneva Conventions dictate that we have water in every interrogation room. We cannot deny it to any prisoner.

"No thank you." He shakes his head and raises his hand, showing me his palm.

"Well, you've probably figured out why we are here." I pause. The 'terp translates my words, and Abu Gamal nods. Before I can continue, he says something in a rapid-fire, staccato tone marred with frequent stutters. The 'terp listens, then translates, "I just want to help. Whatever I can do to help I will do."

"Very good. Thank you. I'm glad you said that, my friend. I want to help you too."

He nods again. As he waits for whatever I'm going to say next, I notice he's folded his hands in his lap. Again, he leans forward. The body language is a "tell"—he's itching to talk.

"Okay, I just want to find out how you came to be captured at the farmhouse yesterday. But before you tell me anything, I want to tell you that I intend to treat you with respect. I expect you to treat me with respect as well."

Abu Gamal hears the translation and breaks into a wide grin. His hands come up, palms open. "I–I will answer any questions. I want to help you." He's obsequious.

"When I ask that you treat me with respect, I mean don't lie to me."

Abu Gamal reacts visibly to this. He shakes his head and assures me he will not lie.

"In return, I'll take care of you. I'll try to help you as best I can."

"Thank you, Mister Matthew." His hands return to his legs. He locks his fingers together and waits, eagerly anticipating my first serious question.

He acts like an innocent person—a bit nervous but wanting to assist. Maybe for once I'll get the truth with direct questioning.

I look into Abu Gamal's eyes—alert, canny, vulnerable—

and ask, "Okay, why don't you tell me why you were at the farmhouse yesterday."

Abu Gamal nods his head repeatedly as he answers, "I–I–I was paid to drive these guys there."

"Who paid you?"

"Uh," he hesitates for a heartbeat before answering, "Abu Raja did."

"Abu Raja? Is he one of the men captured with you in the farmhouse?"

"Y–y–yes. Abu Raja."

"How do you know him?"

"I met him one time through a friend."

"Why did he hire you as a driver?"

"I–I don't know." Hadir mimicks Abu Gamal perfectly. He even duplicates his facial expressions for my benefit.

Abu Gamal's not nervous. This obsequious act is the approach he's running on me.

"How did you know where the house was?"

"Abu Raja knew where it was."

I'm not buying this. I hear Bobby tapping his pen on his notepad, a sure indicator that he's frustrated.

I look suitably astonished as I say, "Okay, let me get this straight. You only met Abu Raja one time, and he asks you to drive him to a house in the middle of nowhere? You weren't worried about where he was taking you? What if it were someplace dangerous?"

Abu Gamal nods eagerly. "No. H–he paid me."

I shift gears, "Tell me about the other guys. There were three others in the car besides Abu Raja, right?"

Abu Gamal leans back in his chair, as if to put distance between us. "Yes. B–but I don't know them."

"You don't know them?" I try to sound surprised.

Abu Gamal nods.

"Okay, you have strangers in your car, you're driving to a house in the middle of nowhere, and you don't bother to ask what's going on or if this might get you in trouble?"

Abu Gamal smiles sadly, as if he'd made a foolish mistake. "No. I–I was just paid to be a driver. That's it."

This is bullshit, and he's distancing. Distancing is a classic resistance technique. A prisoner claims he wants to help, then confesses he doesn't know anyone or anything.

Behind me, Bobby's scribbling away, documenting everything going on in the booth. Hadir opens a can of Coke and takes a sip.

"Where are you from?"

"Baghdad."

"What is your job in Baghdad?"

Abu Gamal hesitates before replying, "I–I own an electronics store."

"Really?" I say. This interests me. "What sort of electronics?"

"I sell . . . stereos, VCRs, TVs, and kitchen appliances."

As I digest this, he adds, "I also do repairs."

I decide to follow up on that later.

"Tell me, how's business right now? Is it good?"

Abu Gamal's hands fly up and he waves one hand quickly from side to side. "N . . . no," he says, "Not good at all. It's actually really bad. It was good until the insurgency started, but then people stopped coming."

"Who's running your shop right now?"

Abu Gamal pretends to think about that for a moment. "My son."

"Your son? Tell me about him. How old is he?"

"He's thirty."

"Is he married?"

"Yes he is." Hadir notes that he sounds mildly disappointed at this.

"Does he have any kids?"

Abu Gamal shakes his head. "No. No children."

Hadir translates this and mirrors his expression.

There's something here. There's a hint of Arab shame in that expression.

"Oh, so you don't have grandkids?"

Abu Gamal matter-of-factly replies, "No. No."

There's no stutter now. Is he hiding something. Or being honest for a change?

"Where does your son live?"

"He lives with my wife and me."

"And your son's wife lives with you as well?"

"Yes."

I decide to press the issue, "And they don't have any kids?"

Abu Gamal again replies matter-of-factly. "No. His wife can't have any." He's dropped his obsequious act. For a second, I see a flicker of disappointment on his face.

"I'm sorry to hear that, my friend."

"She was not my first choice."

I act concerned.

"I'm sorry. Whose choice was she?"

The doppelgänger I'll use with him is starting to take shape.

"My wife's choice," Abu Gamal says with a scowl. Clearly this is an old wound.

"You didn't approve of her as a wife for your son?"

Abu Gamal's lips purse and he expels a burst of air through them. Then he shakes his head, "No. I told my wife that he should marry someone else. But my wife insisted on this . . . this *woman*, and my son married her."

He pauses and looks at the floor. Now he's unable to hide his disappointment. This is a sad subject for him, and he is clearly shamed by it. "She was not a good choice. I cannot have a grandson through her," he adds.

Hadir translates this and imitates Abu Gamal's expression. Hadir confirms my suspicion that Abu Gamal's disappointment stems from the fact that he won't have a male heir to carry on his family's bloodline. It will end with his son.

I'll tuck this away for future use. In the meantime, we need to move on.

I take a sympathetic tone, "I'm very sorry to hear that, Abu Gamal, but perhaps your son will find a second wife someday and give you an heir."

He doesn't sound enthused by this. "*Inshallah*"—God willing—is all he can muster.

"It must be hard to support your family now that your electronics shop is not doing well. How are you getting by?"

Abu Gamal brightens. He leans forward again. The obsequious act returns.

"Well, ac–actually th–that's why I–I was at the house. I–I was paid to drive Abu Raja."

Now we're back to square one. That stutter's back. It's his tell. He's running his approach on me again.

"Whose car did you drive?"

"Mine."

"You've never driven for any of the four other men before?"

"No. N–never."

"When you were in the car, did any of them talk to each other?"

Abu Gamal shakes his head. "No. N–nobody talked."

This is bullshit. He's not volunteering anything. An innocent man would provide more information. A guilty man says little so that he doesn't trip over his own lies. He's involved, all right. But how deeply?

"That's strange. How far is it from your house in Baghdad to the farmhouse?"

"Uh . . . two hours."

"And that whole time, nobody said a word?"

"J–just small talk. Like the weather."

"So who sat up front with you and who sat in back?" This is a key question. We may be able to uncover the hierarchy by finding out who was seated where in the car. I'll compare his response later to what the other four have said. If anyone's lying, we'll know. And, we'll be able to see whom they're trying to protect.

"Abu Raja sat up front with me. The others sat in back."

From behind me, Bobby speaks up, "Was anyone addressed more formally?"

"No."

This is a dead end for now.

I glance back at Bobby, who nods at me. "Tell me, my friend, what happened when you got to the house."

Abu Gamal hears the translation and nods vigorously. "I p–parked in the driveway," his words spew out like machine-gun fire, "The others, they went inside the house. I stayed next to my car and smoked cigarettes."

"Wait, you never went inside the house?"

"No."

Of course, he was found inside the house, and we have photos from the aerial surveillance asset showing that all five went inside.

"You don't know what happened inside the house?"

"Well . . ." He hesitates. For the first time he seems a little unsure of himself. "I–I know now."

"Okay, what happened?"

Again, he pauses. His face is still plastered with the *I want to please you* look that is so transparent now. He's thinking too much, creating a story.

His words come quickly again. "After I heard the h–helicopters come, I ran inside the house."

"So you were inside the house?"

"Yes."

"So you lied to me when you said that you were never in the house."

"Yes," he starts, then quickly adds, "but everything else is true." His head bobs up and down to show how earnest he is now. He's a terrible actor and a bad liar.

"It is not respectful to lie to me."

Silence.

I continue, "What happened inside the house?"

"They told me to go into a room. Abu Raja told us if we got captured, we were to say we were here for a wedding."

"A wedding?"

"Yes."

"Where was the groom?"

100

"I don't know," he replies and bows his head.

"Where was the bride?"

He shrugs his shoulders. "I don't know."

"What, were two men getting married to each other?"

Both Hadir and Abu Gamal chuckle at that. Abu Gamal simply shakes his head.

The levity ends when I ask the next question, "Do you know who else was in the house?"

Abu Gamal listens to the translation and looks at me eagerly.

"No. I h–heard an explosion. I h–heard shooting. Then American soldiers ran into the r–room and blindfolded me."

"Abu Gamal," I begin, "Are you going to act surprised if I tell you that there were five suicide bombers in the house?"

Hadir translates. "I didn't know that." He tries to act surprised, but overdoes it and looks disingenuous instead.

I decide to turn up the pressure.

"Honestly, Abu Gamal, I have to tell you, this is impossible to believe. You are insulting me. I want to help you. I want to get you back to your family. I didn't come to Iraq to break families apart."

Hadir translates. Abu Gamal nods and waits for more.

I lean into him. We're within inches of each other now.

"Obviously, you need to get home to your family. Who's protecting them right now?"

Abu Gamal thinks about that and slowly replies, "I guess my son."

"You need to get back to your family. I want to get you back to your family. But you can't treat me like an idiot. You can't disrespect me with these blatant lies." I've raised my voice now to highlight how frustrated I am with him. "I can't go to my boss and tell him to help you if you're going to lie to me over obvious things."

"But Mister Matthew, I'm not lying! This is true, I swear it!"

"You lied to me about going inside the house!"

"Yes, but everything else . . . I told you the truth! Everything is the truth!"

"Your story is not believable!"

"It is the truth!"

"Don't you want to help yourself?"

"Yes, yes."

I'm entreating him now, "Then you've *got* to let me help you."

Again with the eager-beaver routine, "I w–want to help. I do, Mister Matthew. I will do all I can to help you."

"Then you've got to stop lying to me."

"I am not lying. This is the truth!"

"How long have you known Abu Raja?"

"I met him one time."

"Don't treat me like an idiot."

"Okay. I met him more than once. He is married to my cousin. But everything else I say is truth!"

It's a small crack, but it's a start.

"That's two lies now!" I tell him. He feigns shame.

"What else are you lying about?"

"Nothing, I swear!"

If he's breaking under a little pressure, then it's time to apply more.

Voice stern, I give him the Prisoner's Dilemma, "Look, the other four guys caught with you are being interrogated right now. Whoever starts telling us the truth first will be able to cut a deal. We already know you were in the house—the other guys have told us that. So at least one of them is already talking. You're wasting time by lying. Help me to help you."

Silence. He stares at me hopelessly.

I decide to use Fear Down. We learned this at Fort Huachuca; it's a twist on an old-school, straightforward approach. Show him the true consequences and then give him an out and become his savior.

"My friend, do you know what the penalty is for taking part in suicide bombings?"

He breaks eye contact and stares at the floor as Hadir translates. When the 'terp finishes, Abu Gamal shakes his head.

I reach back to the table and grab a photocopy of the new Iraqi penal code in Arabic. I put it in Abu Gamal's hands, and he looks it over.

"Read line nine."

Abu Gamal reads it aloud. Hadir translates, "Suicide bombings. The punishment for assisting in suicide bombings is death."

"Death."

Silence fills the room. Abu Gamal's eyes meet mine.

He bursts out, "Please. I don't know anything."

"It's not up to me. I don't make the law. I'm just telling you the facts. No court will believe you. If you are convicted, you . . . will . . . hang." I let that reality linger.

His voice rises; he sounds on the edge of desperation, "It's the truth. I was just a driver! I don't know anything! There's nothing I can do about that!"

"Then you will go before the court, Abu Gamal. One

Sunni, one Shia, and one American judge will determine your fate."

The news of this makes Abu Gamal rock back in his chair. He sits bolt upright. His face is plaintive and pleading. "I–I want to help you. I'm not lying. I–I was just p–p–paid to drive my cousin's husband. I–I didn't know there were suicide bombers in the house!"

The pressure is getting to him. He's starting to figure out that the ignorance routine won't work.

"That's not what the others are saying."

"I don't know why!"

"If one of them starts working with us, we won't need you. My boss won't want to cut a deal for information we already have. It will be too late. You will go to Abu Ghraib and stand before the court. Maybe the Sunni judge will believe your story. But the American and Shia judges won't. You and I both know that."

Abu Gamal has no response to this. He looks trapped. Now I turn the old-school approach into a new-school approach. I lean forward and put my hand on Abu Gamal's knee. I give him a smile.

"My friend," I continue, "don't worry. You and I are going to work together. We are friends now. I want to help you. I want to get you home to your family. I understand how difficult it is to live in Iraq right now. You help me, and I'll help you."

For another five minutes, Bobby and I work this angle, but Abu Gamal goes turtle on us. He refuses to budge off his story. He doesn't trust us. Hadir starts to fidget. He needs a cigarette. Abu Gamal's evasive answers have pissed him off. He stands up to stretch his legs and leans against the thin wood wall. To fight off the nicotine withdrawal he chugs the rest of his Coke, then exposes his dull brown teeth with a frustrated smile.

Hadir points out, "He's not saying anything new."

"Abu Gamal," my voice is friendly, "I want you to go think about this meeting. I want you to think about your story. I want you to think about what the other guys captured with you are saying right now. If you cooperate, I'll help you. If not, I won't go out of my way, and you'll be on your own at Abu Ghraib. I want to help you get back to your family."

Abu Gamal's eyes go to the floor. He nods. We call for a guard, who cuffs our prisoner, puts a black mask over his head, and takes him back to the cellblock.

Abu Gamal won the first round. But tomorrow is a new match.

Ten

THE SECOND WIFE

S OMETIMES I THINK of Iraq as a laboratory experiment. The U.S. military came in, shattered the civil order, however brutal, and unleashed chaos instead of imposing order and democracy. As a result, Baghdad in 2006 is a playground for opportunists, thieves, murderers, and fanatics. Caught in the middle are plenty of good people just trying to make a living even as their neighborhoods turn into battlegrounds. Every day, we see the players in this chaos. We see the guilty; we see the blameless. Sorting out one from another is part of our job.

I spend the rest of the day interviewing a farmer and his brother who allowed Al Qaida to hide weapons on their property in return for cash. They are both dry holes and know nothing except that they were paid a few bucks a month to stash guns and ammunition. For them, and for many who fight us, the battle is only about money, not cause or religion or country. Because the economy is in disarray and most average Iraqis can barely sustain their families, they turn to the insurgency to pay their bills. Once the supply of money dries up or the fighting ends, many, including our farmers, will go back to working their land, unconcerned by who won.

Frustrated, I return to the 'gator pit and head for my desk. As I sit down, I notice somebody's put the latest Randyism on the whiteboard.

Kids wear Superman pajamas. Superman wears Randy pajamas.

I bang away on the keyboard, writing up summaries of each interrogation. I get to thinking about Abu Gamal again. The only time he showed any real emotion was when we talked about his daughter-in-law and her inability to bear children. Something's not quite right there; he hasn't told us the whole story yet. I make a mental note to delve into that further tomorrow.

Steve comes into the 'gator pit and sits down next to me. He's an advocate of the new techniques we're spearheading. No one ever taught us to show compassion to our enemies, but this is a natural extension of a criminal investigator's practice. At the interrogations schoolhouse at Fort Huachuca, we learned what army approaches are allowed under Geneva Conventions. But here, in country, we've learned that these methods serve as a launchpad for our own creativity. Each individual is unique, and each approach we design needs to reflect that. We learn, we adapt, we use our knowledge of our enemies' culture against them, we show concern for their well-being, we negotiate. Our new methods are smarter, not harsher. Steve is one of the best at the new methods and at improvising on the fly. In less than a month he's become one of the most respected interrogators in the unit because he gets results.

"Did you break him?" I ask Steve, who has been interrogating Abu Raja, Abu Gamal's cousin-in-law. Break is the jargon we use to signify getting a prisoner to open up a little—like cracking an egg.

"He's getting there," Steve says with a smile. "What about your guy?"

"No, nothing yet," I reply.

"Abu Raja's smart," Steve says, "but he's not too smart. He told me he was in charge of the group. I doubt it. I think he's protecting the bigger fish."

That's a technique we see often when we capture a whole group. The rocks protect the diamonds. It doesn't tell us much, just that they've had some training in counterinterrogation techniques.

"Are you ready to be the head honcho when David leaves?" Steve asks me.

"We've got a good team, and that's all I can ask for," I say.

I do some paperwork then abandon my desk and walk over to the Hollywood room. I find David hunkered down in a broken chair in front of the TVs. I'll be taking over for him as the senior 'gator in just a few days, and he'll head back Stateside to his family. He's looking totally exhausted, and I know he's counting the hours until he can go home. Face drawn, eyes hollow, he's got himself into this state by working fifteen-hour days since he reached Iraq six months ago.

"Hey, David, what's going on?" I ask.

"I just got my ▆▆ chewed by Randy."

Randy is a tough SOB. When you deserve it, he'll praise you and build you up. Many times in our morning meetings, impressed by somebody's work, he'll belt out, "Now that's what I'm ███████ talking about!" But he can be brutal if he discovers you haven't done your homework.

Once one of the younger analysts was supposed to make a few calls to see if one of our detainees was related to another. It slipped his mind, and when Randy asked him about it at the meeting the next morning, the rookie analyst's mea culpa really set Randy off. He shook his head, neck muscles bulging, and bellowed, "I don't GET what's so ███████ HARD about picking UP the goddamned phone and makin' a phone call! GET IT DONE."

The rookie never made that mistake again.

For all his exhaustion, David is always on the ball. He never lets things slip, and I don't think Randy's ever had a problem with him, so this news catches me by surprise.

"What happened?"

David stares at the monitors as if he's in a trance.

Burnt out, hell, he looks defeated. No, not defeated, disillusioned. That's even worse.

"Well, you're going to need to know this, so I might as well tell you."

David has been mentoring me these past few days, trying to get me prepared to be senior interrogator after only three weeks in country. He's about to deliver one of his pearls of wisdom.

"I left Mary off the Group of Five interrogations."

"I noticed that," I reply.

David leans his head back a little but continues to stare at the images on the screens. He's committed to what we're doing here. He's thrown his heart into it. But now he's beaten down and can only muster a hint of frustration.

"Well, I was told that Mary *will* interrogate the top prisoners."

Is somebody short-circuiting our chain of command?

"Isn't it your job to match 'gators with prisoners?"

David's eyes flare with anger. The look disappears, replaced by feigned indifference.

"It's not Mary," he says. "She does fine. But sometimes a woman is not a good fit for a religious guy."

This makes sense to me. Detainees can't pick their interrogator, but sometimes you have to appease them a little to get them to talk. Women bring many advantages to interrogations, but forcing a religious guy to talk to a woman is not going to win him over. This is about getting information, not a conversion.

"Look," David continues, "when you take over, don't get involved in that scene, okay? Be forewarned. You don't have any control over some things."

"Did you tell Randy your thoughts?"

"He said his hands were tied."

I stare at him. In a few days, this headache will be mine.

David sighs and looks up at the ceiling, "This isn't new. Just be careful. That's a fight you can't win."

THE NEXT MORNING, the whiteboard signals David's political defeat. Mary's name sits at the top of the list, scheduled to interrogate Abu Bayda and Abu Haydar, two members of the Group of Five. The analysts suspect Abu Bayda could be a high-level Al Qaida leader because of his evident stature and his poise in the interrogation booth.

In the top right corner of the board, somebody has written, *Randy lost his virginity before his father.*

Cliff and Bobby gather around my desk, and together we go over the game plan for this morning. So far none of the Group of Five has given us anything significant, though Steve has rattled Abu Raja. If anyone cracks today, it'll probably be him.

A few minutes later, Bobby and I sit back down in the interrogation booth. A guard brings in Abu Gamal, and we exchange pleasantries as we did yesterday. This time, though, I want to get right into things, so I keep the small talk brief.

"Have you thought about what I said yesterday?"

Abu Gamal looks tired. He's got bags under his eyes. His mouth is sagging. He doesn't seem as alert as he did yesterday.

"I have."

"You know I want to help you, but first we have to trust each other."

He doesn't answer except to shrug.

"Who are the other men that were caught with you?"

"I only know Abu Raja."

For half an hour, we go over the same ground as yesterday. He won't budge from his story: he doesn't know anybody or anything. I change gears.

"Did you serve in the military?"

Surprised, he replies, "Yes. I was in the army."

"What did you do in the army?"

"I was an electrician. I worked on military vehicles."

"And that's how you learned so much about electronics?"

"That's correct."

Everyone in the room senses where I'm going with this. Abu Gamal looks resolute, but he's unable to hide his anxiety.

"It takes a lot of intelligence and training to be an electrician in the army."

Hadir translate this. Abu Gamal gives an indifferent, "Perhaps."

"Come on," I say, "we both know you're a very intelligent person. We both know what's going on here. We both know what you were doing in the house. Why do you continue to disrespect me?"

"I–I'm s–s–sorry. I don't mean to disrespect you. I just don't know anything."

"How can we believe that? You are a smart guy, Abu Gamal. You have to be smart to work with electronics. And you're trying to tell us that an intelligent guy like you thinks anyone would believe the story you told us yesterday. It's insulting."

As Hadir translates, Abu Gamal tries to look genuinely stricken. As he talks, both hands take flight.

"I didn't m–mean to insult you. I tell you the truth!"

"You lied to me," I say with a disappointed tone.

"I told you the truth!"

"I'm trying to help you, can't you see that?" I'm pleading now. "But first you've got to show me that I can trust you."

He holds to his story. "I want to help you, but I don't

know anything. I don't know the other men. I don't know why we were at the house. I was just a driver."

"A driver who happens to be an electrician."

He has no response to that.

I glance back at Bobby and say, "Van Gogh?"

He nods. "Good idea."

Bobby and I have developed into friendly competitors, attempting creative approaches and ruses. Since Bobby's Zaydan trick, I've been behind him on points. Now's the time to catch up.

I look back at Abu Gamal. He's watching both of us intently. Hadir is in the corner, arms locked together. He wants a cigarette so palpably that it almost makes me want to light up.

I take a deep breath. This one's going to take some acting.

"Okay, my friend, I want you to do me one favor."

Hadir translates. Abu Gamal looks sincere. "Okay," he replies. "Anything. Anything, Mister Matthew. I want t–to help."

Shades of the obsequious mole from yesterday—I might be able to use that against him.

"Close your eyes for me. I'll close mine, too."

Abu Gamal looks puzzled but does as I've asked. After all, he wants to help.

"I want you to imagine looking into your wife's face. You can see your wife's eyes. Her lips, her mouth, her nose, her hair. She's listening to you. See the expression on her face? She is happy to see you. She's smiling. You've filled her with joy."

I take a quick peek. Abu Gamal's eyes are closed. He's concentrating, but he still looks confused.

Hard and fast, like a verbal blow, I say, "Suddenly, the smile's gone! It leaves her face! You're telling her that you've been caught in a house with suicide bombers who were on their way to kill women. And *children*."

I pause for effect.

"You must tell her that you won't ever come home now, that you won't be able to support her. Her eyes fill with tears. She's crying. Her cheeks are wet with tears. Her mouth trembles. She starts to shake. Your words are like daggers stabbing her heart."

I learned this approach from a cagey interrogator back at the schoolhouse at Fort Huachuca. He'd used this on his hardest cases at Gitmo, with some success.

I take a breath and venture another look. Abu Gamal is staring at me, eyes wide. His face is devoid of emotion now.

Before I can say anything further, Abu Gamal turns to look at Hadir. This is unusual. Throughout both interviews, he's maintained eye contact with me.

The two have an exchange. Hadir repeats something. Abu Gamal speaks again, and I can sense a note of surprise in Hadir's response.

At length, Hadir turns to me.

"He doesn't understand which wife he should be imagining."

"He has more than one wife?" I ask.

"Yes," Hadir replies, "he has a second wife."

Islamic law allows men to marry more than one wife. The catch is that they have to accommodate each one equally. This gets expensive fast and makes polygamy financially out of reach for all but the wealthiest men. Abu Gamal doesn't strike me as particularly wealthy.

Why would he hide this? This is significant. I discard Van Gogh and run with it.

Bobby is tapping his pen like an overrevved metronome. He's as surprised as I am.

Say something.

"What's your second wife's name," I ask.

"Farah."

"How old is she?" It's the only thing I can think of to ask. I'm buying time, trying to get a handle on what this means.

Abu Gamal's façade evaporates. He regards me with weary resignation. "She is twenty-two. I married her three years ago."

I've got to find a way to exploit this tidbit.

"That's quite an age difference," I say, allowing it to sound like I'm marveling at his *you-lucky-dog-you* sort of good fortune. Inside, part of me flares with momentary disgust. He could collect Social Security and she's practically a child bride.

Hadir translates this and mirrors my tone of voice. Abu Gamal doesn't look proud.

"Yes, I know. She couldn't get married." A hint of shame breezes across his face. "And I wanted a second wife. It was convenient."

My mind is racing. I'm trying to craft the next question. I'm about to ask him why she couldn't get married. Just as the words reach my tongue. I reel them back. It might offend him, killing the progress we've made.

I switch gears even as my mouth opens, "Uh, why marry a second time, my friend?"

Maybe she wasn't a virgin and that's why nobody wanted her. Asking why she couldn't get married would have made him reveal that, and he's already been embarrassed enough.

Abu Gamal doesn't want to answer this question. For a moment, his look hardens. But his face dissolves in shame again. He mutters something almost under his breath.

Hadir nods, translating: "I wanted to have another son."

The bloodline. He did this to try and perpetuate his bloodline.

As I'm digesting this, Bobby asks, "Does she live in the same house with your first wife?"

Good one. This is a significant question. If she does, that means his first wife approves of her.

Abu Gamal guffaws. "No. If my second wife lived with us, my first wife would kill me."

I can't help laughing at that. Bobby does too, and Hadir grins as well. The pitfalls of polygamy.

Even Abu Gamal chuckles, but he clearly meant what he said.

"I have to put her up in another house. Actually, it is an apartment."

He's just volunteered something for the first time in two sessions. I can feel him moving toward us.

"Where does she live?" I ask.

"The apartment's in Baghdad."

"Is the apartment expensive?"

Abu Gamal shakes his head. "No, it is pretty average."

"Is it expensive to have two wives?" This is, of course, a loaded question.

Abu Gamal listens to Hadir's translation. I notice he's

starting to fidget. He's getting antsy, playing with his hands and fingers.

"M–my s–s–second w–wife," he begins, stuttering severely, "s–she has all t–these needs and wa–wa–wants. It is because sh–she's young. Sh–she likes a lot of th–thi–ngs."

We're circling the truth here. I've got to empathize with him. Play the role. The doppelgänger takes form.

"My wife's the same way," I say sympathetically.

He nods his head. I continue, "She always wants more. If I buy her a ruby, she wants an emerald. If I buy her an emerald, she wants a diamond. If I buy her a diamond, it isn't big enough."

Abu Gamal's eyes light up. He nods vigorously.

████████████████████████████████

"It's never enough. She always wants more, bigger and better."

He nods again. He's stopped fidgeting, and he looks me directly in the eyes. I see hurt behind his. I see a man of good intentions whose been trapped by a bad decision. He's seeking understanding, and I've given that to him. He's grateful.

"Yes . . . yes . . . I know it as well, Mister Matthew. My second wife . . . she loves expensive cosmetics."

"Oh yes, mine as well," I tell him.

Abu Gamal volunteers something else, "Cosmetics, yes, yes. My second wife loves them. The more expensive the better." He pauses, then adds, "And blue jeans. She loves blue jeans as well. Expensive clothes, and jewelry. She is difficult to please."

I nod my head sympathetically. He finishes with a sigh, "She's very expensive."

We're still circling the truth. I push forward.

"Tell me, my friend, it must be very tough on you since your electronics shop isn't doing well."

Abu Gamal goes rigid. With deliberation, he nods his head once. He spears me with his eyes. They don't move from mine as he responds, "Yes, it is. That is why I took this job driving for Abu Raja."

And there it is. Everyone in the booth recognizes it, like a lightbulb just went on over each of us. Abu Gamal has just given us his motive for joining Al Qaida.

Money. He's in it for the money.

I study him. He's still rigid. But I can see in his eyes he knows what he's just said. He knows exactly what he's given us. He's confessed without confessing. He's taken the first step toward us and is gauging our reaction.

It all makes sense now. His shop is circling the drain. His cash-flow situation is getting desperate. His second wife's demand for luxury is insatiable, even in the midst of a war. He cannot continue this lifestyle, yet Islamic law forces him to try.

Then along comes his cousin's husband, Abu Raja, with an offer to make money on the side.

I decide to keep playing the empathy card.

"My friend, I can understand that. It is really hard for Iraqis to make money right now. The American government . . . well . . . we've made many mistakes that have caused the economy to be very bad."

Abu Gamal listens to this and reacts with surprise. He nods lightly in approval. He didn't think an American would criticize his own country.

"Sunnis have lost all their government jobs. The army

was disbanded. There is no law and order. It is very difficult to find work."

"It has been very difficult for us, Mister Matthew."

"And the Shia militias have attacked Sunni neighborhoods and executed many innocent people."

This doesn't have much of an effect on Abu Gamal. He nods without emotion.

He doesn't care about the Sunni-Shia fighting. It isn't a motivator for him. It's all about the money. Cash is the key to him.

"Regular Sunnis like you are having a hard time. I can see why you'd take this job."

"I must provide for my family," he says slowly.

"Yes. That is the most important thing. That's what the Koran says. A man should take care of his family. Nobody would respect you if you didn't care for your family first."

Abu Gamal agrees, and adds, "My first obligation is to my family. That is true."

"My friend, what if you could make some money to help out your family?"

Abu Gamal appears interested, but he is still very cautious. "I just want to help."

I don't know if this is a neutral reply or if he is pulling back into his shell.

"We can help you with your financial needs. But you have to do something for me."

His expression goes blank.

Shit, he's going turtle.

"I'm not going to give you something for nothing. I need to *know* that you are my friend, that you're willing to negotiate in good faith."

He listens, but offers nothing.

Here it goes.

"And the way to negotiate with me in good faith is to tell me about the men you were with. Who are they? What do they do?"

His blank expression solidifies. He's retrenching.

"Mister Matthew," he says, hands out now, trying to look totally genuine, "If I could tell you, I would. But I do not know who they are. I only know Abu Raja."

Now I see fear on his face and I realize that he's afraid of the other four. So he must know or sense how powerful they are. He's still lying.

"I can't help you if you don't trust me. I need something to take to my boss that will show him that you are trustworthy, something that shows you want to help us."

"*Wallah mawf*" (I don't know).

He's back in his shell, and there's no time to try and coax him out again. We still have two more interrogations today.

"Okay, my friend. I understand. I'm trying to help you, but you won't let me. I'm offering you an opportunity to help your family. But you've got to meet me halfway. You can think about this in your cell. I'll see you again tomorrow. Put on your mask."

"I'm sorry." I sense dejection in his voice, like he knows he's doomed no matter what he does.

He picks up the black mask and puts it over his head. A moment later, a guard comes to take him back to his cell.

I look over at Bobby, and we have the same thought. There's $10,000 in cash sitting in our evidence locker. We can use it as bait.

Eleven

A LIFE FOR
REDEMPTION

THE 'GATOR PIT is humming. Interrogators are prepping for their next sessions, huddled with analysts, or talking strategy. The place is never quiet before the first round of interrogations starts. We run two shifts a day and share desks in the small space. Our SF strike teams work day and night to run down the leads we give them. Their helicopters come and go constantly. ███████

███████████████████████████████████

███████████████ The process never ends.

I sit at my desk and contemplate the pile of money in front of me. I've checked out the $10,000 we confiscated in an earlier raid. If I lose it or if it disappears, I will owe ten grand to Uncle Sam.

Today, I'm fishing for Abu Gamal's true motives, and the

cash is bait. We know something about what makes him tick. I plan to test him.

When he takes his mask off, I will pull the money out and toss it on the table Bobby uses to take notes. Ten grand. That's a fortune here, especially for a guy like Abu Gamal. I'm not authorized to give it to him. But I can strongly suggest the stack of bills could be his if only he'd cooperate.

He'll want it.

Or will he?

I think back to a dusty Saudi road I was on a few years ago. I had a backpack slung over my shoulder and a 9mm pistol close at hand. In the backpack was $1 million in cash—payment to a Saudi contractor for work done on behalf of the U.S. Air Force. We were on the way to a bank in Tabuk; there was nobody around for miles except for the contracting sergeant, a retired Saudi colonel, and myself all packed into the colonel's car.

On that deserted stretch of highway, I had a passing thought. With $1 million, I could park myself on a beach somewhere and spend the rest of my life riding the waves, at one with the surf. Two shots, a quick drive to the Jordanian border, and I'd have been gone forever.

But I didn't do it. Why not? I'm no murderer. And money doesn't motivate me. But it motivates Abu Gamal. He'll break as soon as he thinks he can pocket these bills.

I flip through the stack. One hundred $100 bills. They're old and worn, not like the fresh-from-the-mint bundles of cash you see in mob movies. These greenbacks have seen a lot of shady deals.

Why does money motivate Abu Gamal? He's trying to run two households.

I drop the cash down on my desk. I lean forward. My chair squeaks. I cross my arms on my desk and sink my chin onto one wrist. The cash is at eye level now. It is bound by an old, grimy rubber band.

Why does he have that burden? He wanted a male heir.

He married Farah to give him another son, despite the fact that he's on the far side of middle age. At sixty, how could he be a father to his young son? By the time the boy came of age, Abu Gamal would be in his late seventies if he survived that long.

For some, the idea of a teenage bride and a fifty-something groom is just disgusting. When he told us her age and how long they'd been married, I admit I felt a small twinge of repulsion. But doing criminal investigations for the air force had already brought me in contact with the most sordid things imaginable. I once worked an abuse case in which an airman had tortured his infant daughter. Afterwards, he stuffed her in a freezer and closed the door for thirty minutes. I'll never forget having to photograph the latticework bruises on her back that matched the grill shelves in the freezer.

Compared to stuff like that, so what if Abu Gamal had a child bride?

Child bride. He wanted an heir. He wanted his family name to endure. He wanted to preserve his bloodline.

Maybe this wasn't about money after all. We must always distinguish means from ends: This is about his heritage. His family. His pride.

Will this stack of bills work on him? Perhaps. But it's his pride that hangs in the balance, not his savings account.

Behind me, two 'gators kick up a conversation about Iraqi law.

When I brought up the idea of making money from us, Abu Gamal was decidedly noncommittal. He certainly didn't jump at the chance. He didn't see it as a lifeline. Why would actually seeing a bundle of Benjamins induce a different reaction?

The two 'gators continue their discussion. It is loud, and I can't help but overhear parts of it. I try to force their conversation out of my mind. I have to think. I've got to find a way to get inside Abu Gamal's head. Time is short.

We still haven't parsed the connections within the Group of Five. Abu Raja claims to be the leader and has a connection to Abu Gamal. Because Abu Bayda is the oldest and most distinguished, we've tentatively pegged him as the leader. Abu Haydar is the fourth member, and from what I've seen, his mind is like a whippet: fast, sharp, and agile. He's certainly the most cunning of the group.

Why was Abu Gamal so reluctant to tell us about his second wife?

Because he was ashamed. Ashamed by her age? Ashamed by how she's forced him to earn extra money to afford to keep her well stocked in petty luxury items?

Or is it that he feels trapped?

His second wife is spending him into insolvency just as his store is on the brink of failure. His first wife hates Farah. His son cannot give him grandchildren. Farah was his only hope, and instead of producing another son, she's become a terrible burden.

To keep from drowning he turned to Al Qaida for a quick fix to his cash-flow problems. He's not particularly religious. He doesn't seem to have many political convictions. He doesn't hate Shias. He's with Al Qaida simply because there's no other way for him to stay afloat.

How do you trap a man who has already trapped himself? By setting him free.

I wonder how he will react if I offer him exit visas for his entire family. They could start over somewhere else, a new beginning in the sunset of his own life. Would that appeal to him? How proud is he of being an Iraqi? Would he leave his native land?

The two 'gators discussing Iraqi law crank their volume up a notch. Their voices are intrusive and threaten to derail my train of thought. I can't help but listen in.

"How many wives are you allowed under Iraqi law?" I hear one of the 'gators ask the other.

"Four at a time. If you want a fifth, you have to divorce one of your other wives first."

Divorce.

That's Abu Gamal's get-out-of-jail-free card.

Suddenly, I remember an article in an English version of an Iraqi newspaper that announced some reforms to Iraqi divorce law. The new Parliament had changed the laws to make it easier to get one.

I sit up, pull my desktop computer's keyboard forward, and type in a quick Google search for Iraqi divorce petitions.

In a few minutes, I've found a Jordanian divorce petition. I save it to my hard drive and print it out. I'm going to need help to pull this off. I pay a visit to one of our interpreters, a Jordanian who emigrated to the United States back in the nineties. Balding, round-faced, and in his mid-sixties, he is one of the most cheerful people I've ever met.

When I reach his workspace, he looks up at me and flashes a huge grin. "Matt–ew, Matt–ew," he says. He sounds like a mafia don gone Bedouin. "You haf sometin' for me?"

I hand him the divorce petition and explain what I want to do. He beams and says, "I hafta tell yuu, Matt–ew, dis is somethin'!"

He reads through the divorce petition, then turns to his computer. In a few minutes, he's typed it up in Arabic. One more finger to his keyboard, and the printer hums again.

"Thank you Martin."

"I hope dis works, Matt–ew."

Our task force has its own psychological operations unit, composed of four army NCOs. I head over to their shanty, and when I enter, the clutter nearly overwhelms me. Half finished projects litter every table top amid digital printers, printing presses, rolls of posters, and cutting boards. The place looks like a cross between Kinko's and a counterfeiter's lair. These guys could make a fortune if they went under-ground back home. Their forgeries are masterful—nearly imperceptible.

The senior NCO is a clean-cut Midwestern towhead. As with everything else in this office, his appearance is deceiv-ing. He's the cleverest forger we have.

I ask him to affix an official Ministry of the Interior seal on my doctored divorce petition. No problem. In a few min-utes, I have a document that looks like it just came from the MOI itself.

I go find Mustafa, our Iraqi-turned-American entrepre-neur. Years ago, he fled Iraq and settled in Detroit, where he opened a chain of retail stores. Here, he is an interpreter.

Light-skinned, he is a Shia from southern Iraq who returned to help rebuild his country after the 2003 invasion. He and I have had talks about Islam, and when he went home on leave, he returned with two massive Shia versions of the Koran and gave them to me. Each one was the size of a Manhattan phone book. I couldn't believe he'd hauled them all the way from Detroit just for me.

"Mustafa, can you look at this for me and tell me if it looks real?"

He takes it and grabs a chair. Slowly he reads through it, then looks it over again.

"It is very good, but you have the wrong ministry's seal on it."

"What?"

"Divorces are handled through the Ministry of Justice. He'll know that and spot this as a fake."

"I just read in the paper that the MOI is responsible now."

"No. Divorces go through the Ministry of Justice."

What do I do?

Mustafa has never steered me wrong. Yet the newspaper is clear. If I blow this, Abu Gamal will see through my ruse and he'll never trust me. We won't get anything out of him at all.

It has to be right. I don't have time to do any more research. I've got to make a choice: the paper, or Mustafa.

Maybe the news is right. But the change is so recent, most Iraqis won't even know about it yet. Mustafa's right. He'll suspect something if he sees the MOI seal.

I get another copy of the petition, have the psy-op guys

doctor it with the Ministry of Justice seal, and present it to Mustafa again for his scrutiny. He gives it a thumbs-up.

I'm ready to play the game. Just before we go into the booth, I explain my plan to Bobby. He smiles and shakes his head. He knows if this works, I'll catch him on points and he'll have to top me again.

A few minutes later, we're face-to-face with Abu Gamal.

"My friend, how are you today?"

"Hamdulilah." I am fine.

"Are you getting enough to eat?"

"Yes, I have plenty of food to eat."

I can't contain it any longer. My mouth twists upward into a huge grin. For a heartbeat, I just sit there smiling. He looks quizzically at me, but says nothing.

"I have some really good news for you today."

"What is that, Mister Matthew?"

"My friend," I begin as I pull out the divorce petition, "I am about to make you the happiest man in the world."

He looks at the piece of paper, but can't see what it says.

"I'm going to make you happier than the king of Saudi Arabia!"

Hadir breaks out laughing as he translates. Abu Gamal laughs as well. This is the lightest atmosphere we've had with him in the booth. It is a good start.

I hand him the divorce document. Intrigued, he takes it cautiously. Within seconds, he's totally absorbed in reading it. His brow knits. His eyes focus. I've never seen him so intense.

A minute passes. He's still nose-down in the document. A flutter of worry tickles my stomach.

What if he detects it is a forgery? We'll lose any chance with him.

This ruse is a gamble, no doubt about it. I've thrown the dice for this one.

I remain absolutely confident, my smile plastered on my face. I have become the doppelgänger again, the hard-pressed family man with a covetous wife.

Two minutes pass. He flips the paper over and scans the reverse side.

A butterfly kisses my stomach. Then another. I try to ignore them and remain in character, confident, happy. I will give him no clue, not with my actions or body language.

Three minutes now. Abu Gamal gives no hint of what's going on behind those pinpoint eyes of his. His face is frozen in concentration. He rereads the front side again, this time using a finger to mark his place as he goes. His lips quiver as though he wants to read this aloud to himself.

Four minutes go by. He's reexamining the Ministry of Justice seal.

I've thrown the dice. There's nothing I can do now.

Five minutes. Abu Gamal lowers the document. He turns his face to me. It is one big crooked-toothed grin.

"Does this mean I can get a divorce from my second wife?"

I share his smile. Now I'm not acting, I'm elated. The ruse has worked.

"That's exactly what it means," I tell him.

"Allah bless you, Mister Matthew."

"Thank you my friend. We have Iraqi lawyers working here. They'll help you file it and take care of the divorce at no cost to you."

"Thank you, Mister Matthew. Thank you." His face is totally genuine now. The obsequious mole is long gone, crushed by the weight of this gesture.

"Can I fill this out now?" Here sits his path to liberation, and every second is an interminable delay for him.

"Sure. Of course. We can start doing that."

I hand him a pen. He takes it but remains seated. He hesitates for a moment, then locks eyes with me.

"Mister Matthew, may I write a letter to my wife as well?"

"Yeah, that's fine. I'll go get some drinks."

"Thank you, Mister Matthew. Allah bless you."

I walk out through the 'gator pit and grab three Cokes. A few minutes later I return.

"How's it coming?"

Abu Gamal is lost in thought, a few lines of his letter scrawled on the paper in front of him. He jots down a few more sentences, then hands it to Hadir.

"Okay, why don't we take these over to the Iraqi lawyer and get this filed today. Hadir, why don't you come with me."

Bobby stays behind with Abu Gamal.

Hadir and I step outside. "What's the letter say?" I ask. I wonder how harsh he'll be on Farah. Has he explained why he's leaving her?

Hadir looks it over. Without comment, he begins to translate.

My Loving Wife,
You will always be the first star in the night sky, my love. I think of you now, and the memory of your face sustains me.

I am so sorry for everything that I have done. I love you, and always have. You must know that I have been captured.

You have always loved me without reservations, even when I hurt you. I want you to know that I am divorcing Farah. Please, take our son, take all the money, and leave Iraq. Start fresh someplace safe, and remember me. Remember the best times, and forgive me for my mistakes. I beg of you to forgive me.

I would endure ten thousand lashes just to see your face again.

Hadir and I share a shocked moment of silence. He's written a love letter to his first wife, not a breakup one to his second. He's using his one chance to communicate outside this prison to set things right, not to justify his desire for divorce. It is hard not to be touched.

But we still have work to do. I leave the divorce petition and the letter on my desk. Hadir and I return to the booth and sit down. Now comes the payoff—we hope.

"Look, my friend. I've done this for you because I think you are a decent person. I understand why people are doing the things they are in Iraq. You don't have many choices."

Abut Gamal shakes his head sadly. "No, we do not."

"You have to support your family. I'm a family man, too and know I'd do the same thing. I'm not here to judge you."

Abu Gamal agrees with me, "Family is important."

"I've done something for you. Now I need you to do something for me."

"*Inshallah.*"

"All I'm asking you to do is tell me the obvious. Tell me the things we already know."

Abu Gamal replies with a curt nod. I just want him to

start talking, start telling me the truth of what happened at the farmhouse.

"Are you ready?"

"Yes I am ready."

"Tell me why you were at the farmhouse."

Without the slightest hesitation, Abu Gamal replies, "I was there to make the suicide vests."

His confession carries no emotion.

He's the bomb maker.

"Did you make all of them?"

No hesitation, "Yes I did."

Inside, I'm jubilant. Outside, I'm calm and matter-of-fact. Nothing fazes me.

How much can we get? How far will he go?

"Why were the other people at the house?"

He shakes his head, "I don't know. I really don't."

Is he still protecting the others? If so, why? His confession is more than enough to send him to the hangman's noose.

"But you made the vests?"

"Yes."

"Did you bring the explosives?"

"No, they were already at the house." He pauses after that revelation. I can see he's thinking, trying to decide how far he wants to go.

In for a dollar. . . .

"I wired the vests. That is my job."

Electrician in the army, stereo salesman as a civilian, he's turned to bomb-making to earn a living in wartime.

"My friend, have you made other vests?"

He waves a hand. It is almost a dismissive gesture. "Yes. I've made many."

"Have you made other things besides vests?"

He looks down at the floor, takes a breath and replies, "Yes. I've made roadside bombs as well."

"What about car bombs?" I ask.

"No. I did not work on those. I worked on the wiring for the roadside bombs. Sometimes, I would build in a transistor or a unique detonator system."

"What did you use for that?"

"Garage door openers, stereo remote controls, and cell phones. I never worked with the explosives. Just the wiring."

"How many bombs have you built?"

His face is dead as he answers, "Hundreds."

"Hundreds?"

"Yes. Hundreds."

That could be over a thousand victims. Americans and Iraqis. He's a mass murderer.

"How much do you get for this work?"

"Fifty dollars per job."

Thousands dead so his wife could wear lipstick, blue jeans, and bling.

"I can understand that. You needed the money."

"Yes, I have . . . had . . . two wives to support. I want you to know Mister Matthew, I did not plant the bombs. I just built them."

"I understand. If you didn't build them, then someone else would have."

"Yes, Mister Matthew. I just helped make them."

"I understand." I nod very slightly. I'm very careful

with my nonverbal cues. I want my sympathy to seem genuine.

"So you went to the farmhouse to wire the suicide vests."

"Yes."

We've got to get him talking about the Group of Five. I want to see how far this break will take us.

"Abu Gamal, how long have you known Abu Raja?"

His right hand comes up to his chin. He's deliberating.

"I have not known him that long."

Damn. I thought he'd tell us something new.

"But you've done all these vests," I interject.

He remains silent. Behind his eyes I see a new emotion. Defeat. Abu Gamal knows what he's just done. He's given up his own life. That was his only asset in this negotiation. He's confessed, and he knows he will hang now. But his desire to honor our deal as well as his sense of obligation to his wife, his true love, propels him to continue giving us information.

"Who else were you working with?"

"I would get assignments, but I would not know the people."

Usually, by this time Hadir is in dire need of a smoke. This afternoon, he's riveted.

"Where would you go to do the work?"

"Different places. I can't remember."

I won't let him go back in his shell.

"Okay, just tell me one place you went. You must remember one place."

"No. I didn't know where I was."

"Tell me about Abu Raja."

"I've told you all I know already."

He knows that if he talks, Al Qaida will kill his wife and son. He'd rather die than let that happen.

"My friend, where did you go? Would Abu Raja tell you where to go?"

"Sometimes. I would get assignments, but I wouldn't know the people. They would either pick me up or have a taxi come to get me."

"Okay, just tell me one place, any place, where you built a bomb."

"I don't remember."

He's made himself the sacrifice here, but he's protecting everyone else. I don't want to get frustrated with him. He's already come far in this session and I don't want to drive him away. I must use what little trust I've won.

"My friend, I helped you get a divorce, and now I'm asking you to help me. You must be able to remember at least one place. One place where you put together vests. I need something."

Abu Gamal considers this. He strokes his patchy beard, fingers on his chin. He is staring at me, sizing me up. And then he talks.

"Okay."

We wait. Bobby starts tapping his pen. Hadir crosses his arms.

"Th–there was this house, an apartment . . ."

His stutter is back. Is he nervous? Disingenuous? I can't tell.

"Where was this house?"

"Apartment."

"Yes, apartment."

"It was in a small town in Yusufiyah."

"If I show you a map, will you show it to me?"

A deep breath. His eyes roam. There's no escape, not now.

"My friend, I did something for you. I helped you. Now I'm asking you to help me. It's just one place."

"Okay, I will show you."

I fire up the laptop on the table and bring up a digital map on the flat-screen TV on the wall. With Abu Gamal's help, we navigate from Baghdad to the Yusufiyah countryside and make our way over the Euphrates River to a small village. Abu Gamal strains to read the map but then recognizes a soccer field and from there points out the apartment that he visited. It's third in a row of white two-story buildings. It'll be our next Special Forces target.

"Abu Raja would tell me to go to places, such as this one, then he'd pay me."

"You've never seen the other four men before?"

"No. This was the first time I worked with them."

"You drove together, the five of you in your car?"

"Yes."

"Who spoke in the car?"

Hesitation. His eyes find the floor. He's frowning now. Either he's thinking about what to give us, or he's going to give up.

"Abu Raja and Abu Haydar spoke to each other."

That's something. Press it.

"Did Abu Haydar speak formally with Abu Raja?"

"No, he spoke informally to him."

That's a big clue. Abu Haydar is at least Abu Raja's equal. We know that now.

"Who was in charge?"

Abu Gamal doesn't respond.

"My friend, I can protect your family. No one will know it came from you."

"I'm sorry, I cannot help you further, Mister Matthew. I have to think of my family."

He knows I can't protect them.

For another hour, we try to coax a few more details out of Abu Gamal without success. Finally, I see we're not going to get anything else out of him. It is time to end our relationship.

"My friend, I will do what I can to help you. But you have not talked about the others, so what I can do is limited."

"I know. Thank you, Mister Matthew. I cannot help further."

With those words, Abu Gamal retreats inside himself again. I suspect he has no loyalty to Abu Raja and the others. He doesn't care about their cause. It's fear for his family that keeps him from breaking wide open.

I wish him luck. He stares at me in despair. "Good-bye, Mister Matthew. Thank you for helping me."

He puts on his black mask, and the guard comes to retrieve him. Bobby, Hadir, and I return to the 'gator pit and pass on the apartment's location to Captain Randy. He gives us an *Attaboy* and immediately heads over to see the Special Forces commander. By the time I finish drafting my report of the interrogation, I can hear their helicopters spinning up on the launchpads a hundred meters from the front door.

Meanwhile, Abu Gamal's fate is sealed. He'll soon be transferred to Abu Ghraib and will ultimately keep his date with the prison's executioner.

I hear Special Forces helicopters lift off the pads. I pick up Abu Gamal's divorce petition and the letter to his wife.

Abu Gamal traded his life for a chance to seek forgiveness from his beloved wife. He gave himself up to get this letter out and set right his mistakes. He thought the divorce decree liberated him from Farah and all the trouble she caused him.

But the letter—I could get it to his wife. I could slip it in the mail. I have her address. The Iraqi postal service does work. I'm tempted to do it because I feel empathy for him. He tried to redeem himself and he helped me.

Hundreds. He made hundreds of bombs.

Women. Little kids. Old men. Merchants. Customers. Friends. Neighbors. They were all blown to pieces—for what? Because a stereo salesmen got himself in a bind and couldn't afford his second wife's appetite for the good life.

He traded his soul for jeans and jewelry. He traded his life to undo the damage with his wife but never once showed remorse for the people he'd helped to kill. The doppelgänger that grew out of our relationship dies with that realization. I am me again, the major with an obligation—not to a wife or children but to the victims of those bombs. They are the reason I volunteered to come to Iraq.

Interrogators are not meant to be arbiters of justice. We simply gather information. The court at Abu Ghraib metes out punishment, and the distinction is clear and inviolable.

Except this one time.

I rise from my desk, letter and divorce petition in hand.

The Special Forces helicopters thunder overhead, speeding for Yusufiyah and the target Abu Gamal has given us.

He is a mass murderer who loved his wife. That one human connection does not redeem him in my eyes. He forfeited that right the first time he wired a vest. Certainly his victims, dead or maimed beyond recognition—the shattered limbs, the torn and bloodied faces—did not receive mercy. Abu Gamal may not have been motivated by money but he was still a barren human being.

I decide to deny him his shot at redemption.

The sound of the Blackhawks ebbs and the bustle of the 'gator pit surrounds me.

Into our shredder I feed Abu Gamal's last hope. The shreds fall into a wastebasket, anonymous and soon forgotten.

Twelve

PREACHER OF HATE

R ANDY IS MORE agitated at the morning meeting than usual. The task force commander called earlier looking for an update and found his report wanting. We're falling behind, and the attacks in Baghdad increase daily.

No pressure or anything.

We begin to go through the detainees we have in the prison. The eleven o'clock meeting allows the previous shift to tell the oncoming shift—'gators, analysts, and support personnel—what's been accomplished in the previous twelve hours. Today, the mood is somber. Aside from Abu Gamal, we haven't had much luck.

Photos of Abu Bayda and Abu Haydar flash up on the flat-screen at the front of the room. Lenny stands.

"Neither of them are talking," he tells us.

Randy mutters *damn* under his breath.

"Recommendation?" Randy asks.

Lenny thinks about it.

"Retain and exploit both."

"Agreed."

Randy turns to the flat-screen at the front of the room, and Abu Raja's face appears.

Nathan stands up; Steve, who's been working with Nathan on my shift, stays seated next to him.

"Detainee provided no targets, but we're close. He's pretty worn out. We're going to run a new approach on him today and continue to hit him with the information that Abu Gamal provided."

"Good. For God's sake, get something out of him."

Randy stands, puts a foot up on his chair, and leans with an arm on his knee.

"Let's look at what we have here people. We've got five well-dressed guys in a farmhouse full of suicide bombers. One's admitted to being the bomb maker. The other four are still sticking to the *I don't know* ▆▆ story. They all have different excuses for being at the house, and none of them adds up. They concocted that line ▆▆▆▆▆ on the fly, just before our team entered the house. We know what they were doing at the house, but we don't know who they are or how they fit into Al Qaida's network. But at least three of them—Abu Bayda, Abu Raja, and Abu Haydar—are big fish. We've got to figure this out, okay? As of now, these three guys are the top priority. We've got to be relentless. We're close, I can feel it."

Steve and Nathan nod. They sense it, too. There's something about the Group of Five that has all of our instincts buzzing.

"Okay, moving on. We've got some personnel changes Bobby's leaving us to go to an outstation."

My heart sinks. Bobby and I have a rhythm going.

"Also, as you know, this is David's last day. Matthew's our new senior interrogator. That's it."

The meeting breaks up and those people getting off shift exit the room. My shift of interrogators stays behind, waiting for me to give them their assignments based on Randy's priorities. I match up the detainees with the 'gators on my team and then read out the assignments. After I finish, I go to the whiteboard and draw out the assignments with a marker.

I see that someone has already put up a Randyism for the day. *There is no theory of evolution. Just a list of creatures Randy has allowed to live.*

Steve and Cliff are discussing strategy for the next round with Abu Raja. Abu Gamal has given us enough information to use our We Know All approach. I can't wait to watch Steve in action from the Hollywood room. He's built up a rapport with Abu Raja and now he's going to try and cash it in.

Twenty minutes later, Abu Raja sits across from Steve in the interrogation booth, his knees locked together and his hands dug deep into the tight space between his legs. He hunches slightly, and his toes turn inward on the concrete floor. He looks totally drained. Steve, on the other hand, is full of vitality. He starts off with small talk and then begins asking questions.

"We know you weren't in the house to film a wedding, Abu Raja. So let's not begin with that today, okay? It's insulting."

Abu Raja mumbles something. The microphone in the room doesn't pick it up, and in the Hollywood room, I turn up the volume on my headset. Abu Raja has a maddening habit of talking very quickly under his breath. He needs no 'terp because he speaks fluent English with a slight British accent. He's one of the best-educated Iraqis we've seen here at the compound.

"What did you say?" Steve asks.

Abu Raja runs a hand over his bald head. He has tufts of unruly black hair cresting his skull at ear level as though middle age has given him a reverse mohawk.

"I said, I'm very sorry sir. I will help you if I can."

"Okay, good. What were you doing at the farmhouse?"

"I was there to attend a wedding."

Steve gets pissed at this answer, "That's bullshit and you know it. You think I'm an idiot?"

"No. No, sir. I didn't mean any disrespect."

"Good. Look, you know we found you in a house with five suicide bombers."

No answer.

"And you know what the punishment is for that under Iraqi law, right?"

Abu Raja looks morose—no, he looks absolutely lost. He answers, "Yes. Death."

"I don't want to see you die. You're a good guy, Abu Raja. Iraq needs your skills as a doctor. It would be a tragedy to lose them."

No response. His frown grows long. I wonder if he's going to cry. He pulls a sweaty hand from between his legs and adjusts his glasses. His eyes stay fixed on the floor.

"How long have you been a pediatrician?"

"Ten years, sir."

"Do you like being a doctor? Working with kids?"

"Yes. Very much."

"Wouldn't you want to get back to your real calling?"

"Yes, sir. But I know that's not going to happen."

"Not necessarily. If you help us, I will help you."

Abu Raja nods.

"Last time we talked about your mother."

"Yes, sir."

"Where is she?"

"We live in Baghdad."

Genuine concern fills Steve's voice.

"Who is looking after her right now?"

"Nobody, sir." Abu Raja's voice cracks as he replies.

"I know you said your father died when you were young, but tell me again, how did he die?"

Abu Raja rocks backwards and plunges his hand back between his legs.

"I was ten. He was a soldier. The Iranians captured him. After three years, he died in their prison." The Iranians were notorious for torturing Iraqi prisoners of war.

I adjust my headset, turn the volume up a little more, and scoot my chair closer to the monitor. The camera is focused right on Abu Raja's face. His expression is pained. He's not going to last long against Steve.

"I am sorry to hear that. You must not like what Iran is doing to your country now, then."

Bitterly he replies, "They arm the Shia against us. The death squads. The militias."

"Iraq has suffered many hardships."

"Yes."

"You have suffered many hardships."

"Yes."

"So has your mother."

No response.

144

"Let me help you. We want to work with you Abu Raja. We want to build a strong Iraq."

His head slowly lifts. His eyes settle on Steve at last.

"Yes, sir."

"Tell me the truth. What were you doing in the house? But wait—before you answer, you need to know something."

"What?"

"We know you're married to Abu Gamal's cousin."

Shock registers on Abu Raja's face.

"The others have been talking. If you want to cut a deal with us, if you want us to help you, now's the time. We know almost everything, thanks to the others. So be honest with me, okay?"

Abu Raja slowly nods. He knows the jig is up.

"Good. What were you doing in the farmhouse?"

"I was told to go there by a friend." Finally, he's given Steve something.

"Who is your friend?"

"Yes, sir. A friend."

"What is his name?" Steve sounds slightly frustrated.

Abu Raja picks this up as well.

"His name is Abu Shafiq."

I lean back in my chair and whisper, "Attaboy, Steve. Keep him talking."

"Why did Abu Shafiq want you at the farmhouse?"

"He did not say, sir."

"My friend," Steve says. "The truth."

"I tell you the truth."

"Did you know you would be meeting suicide bombers there?"

Desperation suffuses Abu Raja's voice, "I did not know about any suicide bombers."

"I don't believe that. You're insulting me again."

"I am sorry, sir. I am sorry. I was just told by Abu Shafiq to pick up Abu Haydar."

"Why?"

"To videotape a wedding."

"A wedding?"

"Yes, sir."

"Who is Abu Shafiq?"

"A friend."

"Where do you meet him?"

"At the Mansur Mosque. Or sometimes we meet at a falafel stand."

"Will you show me on a map?"

"Yes."

Steve brings up a map using the laptop computer on the table and the flat-screen television on the wall. Abu Raja studies it and picks out a street corner used by the falafel stand.

"Is Abu Shafiq a friend, or is he your boss?"

A long pause. This is the moment. He's going to break, I can feel it. Steve's brought his A-game.

"My boss."

The reward poster. A reward of $10,000,000 was offered for information leading to Zarqawi's capture. No reward was ever paid.

On February 22, 2006, members of Al Qaida in Iraq blew up the Golden Mosque in Samarra, also known as Al Askari Mosque, one of the holiest Shia shrines. The destruction incited a civil war between Sunni and Shia.

3

From the video captured at Naji's house showing Zarqawi unable to reload a M249 semiautomatic weapon. This unedited footage was released by Coalition Forces to discredit Zarqawi.

4

Zarqawi delivering his message of intolerance. From the same video.

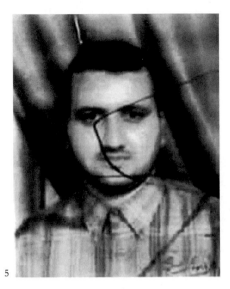

Sheikh Abu 'Abd al Rahman, Zarqawi's spiritual advisor, and Abu Haydar's lifelong friend.

5

6

The air strike on Zarqawi's safe house. U.S. Air Force F-16s dropped two 500-pound laser-guided bombs on the house.

7

The remains of Zarqawi's safe house.

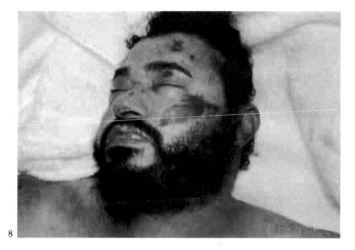

The deceased Zarqawi.

Iraqi soldiers celebrating the news of Zarqawi's death.

10

The new leader of Al Qaida in Mesopotamia,
Abu Ayyub al Masri.

11

The author. Taken at Baghdad International Airport
in April 2003.

The author.

Now we have the next rung on the ladder to Zarqawi.

"Tell me about him."

"I know nothing about him. I've told you everything I know."

Steve changes approaches.

"Abu Raja, you're a very intelligent man."

"Thank you, sir."

"Why give up your career and join Al Qaida?"

No response.

"Come on, be honest."

Abu Raja's hands come out from between his legs. For once he sits confidently and looks Steve straight in the eye.

"The Iranians use the Shia to kill us. The Shia take our jobs away. They kidnap our people. They terrorize our neighborhoods. Every day, I see friends disappear only to turn up dead days later. They bind their hands. Torture them."

He holds back tears and anger. Steve's compassion is remarkable. He reaches out and touches Abu Raja's knee.

"You Americans don't stop this. You let this happen. People like me, we had no choice. Only Al Qaida offered us hope. Only Al Qaida came to help us."

"We want to work with you, Abu Raja."

The bitterness returns, "You *caused* this."

"Why did you go to the house?"

Abu Raja sounds exasperated, "Because I was told to go there by Abu Shafiq."

"To do what?"

"I was just told to pick up Abu Haydar so he could videotape."

"Okay, we're going in circles here. I can't help you unless

you help me. I'm out of time for today. Let's talk again to-morrow."

"Yes, sir."

A guard retrieves Abu Raja and takes him away. A few minutes later, Steve and I meet in the 'gator pit. Cliff comes over, and the three of us dissect the intelligence. Abu Raja's given us our first lead upward from the Group of Five. Now we know their boss. If Abu Shafiq can assemble a group of suicide bombers with educated Iraqis then he must have power and control. He's got to be only one or at most two steps removed from Zarqawi. The trail is hot again.

Thirteen

THE BLUE BMW

S INCE THE SECOND Battle of Fallujah, Ramadi has
been a key Al Qaida stronghold in Anbar Province. It
is rumored in intelligence circles that Al Qaida leadership in the operational wing has taken root there. Every
day, marines and army units see action, both in the streets
and on the outskirts of town. Nowhere is safe.

In mid-April, a firefight erupts in the city proper. The insurgents hold their ground, blasting away at our troops with
AK-47s. Two insurgents die, their bodies crumpling to the
pavement. In the middle of the battle, a blue BMW 325 races
through the streets and screeches to a halt in front of the
corpses. Two men jump out of the car. Other insurgents run
to the vehicle and load the bodies into the trunk. AKs are
thrown in on top of the corpses. Before anyone can react, the
car burns rubber and races away from the scene.

A Kiowa scout helicopter circling above the firefight ob-
serves the entire scene. The pilot flips on a video camera,

then gives pursuit, tracking the BMW to an apartment complex a few miles from the firefight. A raid team kicks in a door and catches three men, all brothers. Problem is, they've stashed the weapons and hidden the bodies. A thorough search of the complex fails to find them.

The brothers are brought to us, and Randy asks that we make them our priority. The troops in the field need to know where the bodies went and where the guns are hidden. I take the oldest brother, whose name is Yusif. Steve gets the middle one. I assign another 'gator on my team, Marcia, to the youngest.

Before I head into the booth, I read the screener's report on Yusif. Our screener is a senior army NCO who couldn't cut it as an interrogator. Somewhere along the way, somebody told him that insurgents can be identified by their dirty, earth-encrusted hands. It has become a running joke among the interrogators that every screening report he writes includes detailed descriptions of the detainee's fingers, palms, and nails. This time, our screener reports Yusif's hands are girlishly soft. He has no calluses, and his hands are clean. Of course, this means nothing; it could be that he wears work gloves while digging holes for IEDs.

I head into the booth to meet Yusif. He speaks little English, so Mustafa, our 'terp, joins us.

Yusif sits down in one of the white plastic chairs and removes his mask. I'm startled by his appearance. He's light-skinned, almost white, and has pale blue eyes. He doesn't look like a typical Iraqi at all.

It's time to see what sort of character I have in front of me. Use rapport and small talk to find out what shape the doppelgänger needs to take.

I introduce myself. Yusif seems cordial enough but very scared. I start with the basics.

"Where are you from?"

"Ramadi."

"You've lived in Ramadi all your life?"

He turns to look at the interpreter as Mustafa translates this. I ask him to keep his eyes on me.

"I am sorry. Yes. I have lived in Ramadi all my life."

"What do you do for a living?"

"I am a cameraman."

BMW in a firefight. Cameraman. The picture's starting to come into focus.

"Who do you work for?"

Yusif pats his shoulder, "I work for myself. I freelance."

"Really? For who?" I'm very interested in this and make no effort to hide it. I notice that Mustafa mirrors my tone when he translates this.

Yusif answers matter-of-factly. He's starting to calm down a little. His initial fear is giving way to caution.

"I videotape weddings mostly."

Here we go again. █████████████████████
████████

He says something else. I resist the urge to look at Mustafa, who says, "I also videotape birthday parties and sports for the local news. Soccer mainly."

"So you're a journalist?" I ask.

"Not really. But I have sold film to *Al Arabiya*."

"What sort of film?" Every instinct is humming. This guy could be out filming those gruesome beheading videos and executions Bobby showed me.

"Soccer matches. Just sports, really."

"Have you ever filmed anything about the war?"

"No." Flatly and speedily answered.

"Who do you live with? Are you married?"

Yusif replies; Mustafa translates. "I'm not married. I live with my two younger brothers and my mother. I support them. My father died in the war against Iran."

Ping. A reason to hate Shia.

"How is business for you?"

I'm thinking about Abu Gamal. Maybe his freelance work dried up, and to make ends meet he started filming for Al Qaida.

"Not good. We're not rich, but at least we are surviving. My brothers work manual labor jobs to supplement my income."

"I imagine it is difficult to do your job these days."

"Yes. It is very dangerous to be out. But we get by."

I try to look as sympathetic as possible as I ask the next question.

"Yusif, do you know anyone affected by all the violence in Ramadi?"

"Yes. A friend of mine last month."

Mustafa waits for him to continue. When he doesn't, I prod him. "What happened?"

"He was a journalist. Somebody kidnapped him."

Yusif speaks a few more sentences, then waits patiently for Mustafa to translate. His eyes are watery. Clearly this was not an easy question for him to answer.

"My friend was found beheaded. Whoever kidnapped him tortured him with a drill. He had marks from it all over his body."

There's motive for joining Al Qaida right there. The same

motive these other Sunni have had: protection from the Shia militias.

I decide to work this angle a little longer.

"That must have been hard, Yusif. I am sorry."

Mustafa looks very grim as he listens to Yusif's reply.

"Yes it was. I saw him at the morgue. He . . . was . . . without . . . his head. I went with his mother. It was horrible. They did terrible things to my friend."

The doppelgänger starts to take form. Sympathy. Understanding. Those will be the weapons I use next.

"It must have made you very mad to see this. I'd want to take up arms and defend my people from this horror."

Yusif shakes his head slowly. He looks desperately sad. "Perhaps. But I don't think the answer is meeting violence with violence."

Yusif, what are you? Martin Luther King, Jr.? You're minimizing here, backing away from my bait. My question was too obvious. My mistake.

He continues. "I am out a lot. I have seen bodies. I don't like where Iraq is going, and the insurgent groups aren't helping. They are not the answer. The only way is peace."

Now he's running an approach on me. I need to regain the initiative. I decide to switch gears.

"Do you own a car?"

"Yes, I have a blue BMW 325."

"That's a nice car."

"Yes it is."

"With money so tight, how can you afford it?"

Yusif shrugs. "Actually, we can't afford it. I haven't driven it for over a month. We have no money for gas."

"That's interesting."

"Why is that?" he asks me, puzzled.

I decide to lay one of my cards on the table.

"Well, would it surprise you to know that your car was seen in another place earlier today?"

Yusif reacts with surprise. His eyes grow slightly wider. "Yes, it would. It would surprise me a lot. In fact, that is not possible."

"Why do you say that?"

"My brothers and I were home all day with my mother. The car didn't move from our parking space."

I decide to keep him off balance and hit him with another line of questioning. Retain the initiative.

"Your mother is at home?"

"Yes." His expression turns from cautious to worried. I've hit a nerve.

"She's by herself?"

"Yes."

"You must be very concerned for her."

"I am. And I know she is very worried for us."

"I am concerned for your mother as well. These are dangerous times. She shouldn't be alone."

He nods but doesn't answer. I decide to offer him a deal.

"Let's get you out of here so you can return to her."

He looks relieved. "I would appreciate that very much."

"I have to tell you though, the only way that will happen is if you're honest with me."

"I will tell you the truth. Whatever you need to know, I will tell you."

He sounds like Abu Gamal.

"When was the last time you drove the BMW?"

A lightbulb goes on in his brain. I can see him realizing

154

that this is why he's here. We have something on him and his car.

"The car hasn't moved in the last month," he replies a little too quickly.

"Not a good start Yusif. We know the car has moved. You've got to at least be honest about that."

"No! I swear, it hasn't moved."

I shake my head sadly. "Think of your mother, Yusif. Why do you lie to me?"

Mustafa injects Yusif's pleading tone into his translated answer, "I am not lying. Please, you must believe me."

Before I left the 'gator pit, Cliff gave me two still photographs taken from the Kiowa's video recording of the incident. One shows the BMW parked in front of Yusif's apartment. The other shows it in the firefight with the bodies being loaded into the trunk.

I pull the first one out of my notebook and hand it to Yusif. "Is that your car?" I ask him.

"Yes." He sounds nervous now.

I hand him the second photo. "Is that your car?"

He studies it. His hands start to shake. He stutters an answer. Mustafa says, "Yeah, it looks like mine. When was this taken?"

"It was taken a few hours ago during a firefight in Ramadi."

Yusif hears this and goes polar white. He looks like a corpse. He stutters another answer, shaking his head at the same time. His hands shake even worse. "No. That's impossible. I was home all day and the car never moved."

I am sick of going in circles with this guy.

"That's ridiculous. The evidence is right here!" I slap a

hand on the photographs. "Could your brothers have taken the car without your knowing it?"

"No! I have only one set of keys! I had them with me all day."

I'm going to turn the screws on him and then transform this into a new-school approach. I've got to get him past this line of crap.

"Now you're just insulting me."

When Mustafa translates this, Yusif's eyes become saucers. "No, I tell you the truth. I swear!"

"Then explain these!" I nearly shout, holding up the photographs.

"I can't. It looks like my car in the second photo, but mine has not moved."

This is going nowhere, so I change my approach.

I calm down and for a good twenty seconds I don't say anything. I switch my gaze from the notepad back to Yusif. He looks absolutely miserable.

"Yusif. Think about your mother for a minute. I want you to close your eyes and imagine her face."

Reluctantly, he closes his eyes.

"Picture your mother's face and how worried she is. Can you see the expression on her face? She is home alone in a city overwhelmed with violence. How will she get food? How will she pay bills without your income? How can she survive without you and your brothers? Where are her sons that were just taken by the Americans? She must be asking herself questions right now."

Yusif hunches forward, keeping his eyes squeezed closed. A single tear escapes his right eye and streaks down his cheek.

"I'm not blaming you for doing anything," I say softly. The change in my tone causes him to open his eyes and watch me. With one sleeve, he wipes the tear away.

He's going to buy this. I know it. So I press.

"I'm not even mad that you were out there today in that fight. You probably needed money, and after all, you didn't shoot at Coalition Forces. All you did was pick up the bodies and move some guns. And given what the Shia militias are doing to Sunni all over Iraq, I understand why you'd feel compelled to take up arms. You have to defend yourself and your family."

Nailed it. He's going to break. I can feel it.

"So, I'm going to help you and your brothers. I'm going to make sure that at the very least, we get your younger brothers back to your mother as soon as possible. But you have got to give me something."

His head drops. He studies the floor. He's crying now. He manages a short response. Mustafa looks frustrated as he gives me Yusif's reply, "We were home all day."

Damnit! Okay, I'll have to let the doppelgänger come into better focus

"You're the oldest, right?"

"Yes."

"You've taken care of your brothers and your mother since your father died, right?"

"Yes. That is my responsibility." His voice is just a hoarse whisper now.

"I know it is your responsibility. I am the oldest brother in my family. I know it is my job to look after my younger brothers. You know that lying to me isn't going to help your brothers. I can't get them released if you keep lying."

He shakes his head. Twice. Three times. It is an odd gesture, like he's trying to awake from a nightmare. "The car never moved. It never moved. I am telling the truth."

He's gone turtle, and I'm running out of time for this session.

I pull out two more photos from my notebook. They are prison mug shots of Yusif's brothers. I show them to Yusif. The sight of his brothers in orange jumpsuits leaves him overwhelmed.

"Take these," I order. "Take them back to your cell. Look at them tonight. Think about your responsibility to them. Think about the truth. The car. The evidence we have. We'll talk tomorrow."

I try to hand the photos to him, but his hands quake so badly he can't grab them. I lean forward and fold them into his jumpsuit's breast pocket. His voice cracks. He tries to say something. Mustafa asks him to repeat it.

"I am telling the truth."

"Put your mask back on."

His hands tremble so badly that I have to help him get it over his head. A guard comes in and leads him back to his cell as I head for the 'gator pit. I'm angry and frustrated. This guy is a diversion from our real mission. Cracking Yusif and his brothers won't get us closer to Zarqawi. They're small fry, foot soldiers in the battle. We need to be focusing on the big fish like the remains of the Group of Five.

On top of that, his story is so ridiculously transparent that I'm shocked he wouldn't concoct a better one to cover for his brothers. If it were my own brothers, I'd be doing everything I could to protect them.

I meet up with Steve. We compare notes. Turns out, the

middle brother also says the car hasn't moved in a month. They must have had just enough time to create a legend before the raid team grabbed them.

"Why leave your brothers hanging like that," I muse.

Steve can't believe it either, "Yeah. Pretty stupid, isn't it."

Anger swells in me. "Tomorrow is going to be a lot harder on him."

Fourteen

THE DEVIL'S CHOICE

T HE NEXT MORNING I pause outside the booth. I take a deep breath and exhale away my identity. Another breath, and I start to change back into the doppelgänger. No longer the youngest in my family, no longer an American who sees the Sunni and Shia violence as the ultimate expression of intolerance and ignorance, I become something else. I am sympathetic to the Sunni who live with the constant threat of terror. I am the oldest brother freighted with the same burdens as Yusif. I am Yusif's friend.

I step into the booth. Mustafa awaits me there. A moment later, Yusif comes in and is eased into his white plastic chair. I can't help but feel a little contempt for him as I watch him take off his mask. He stuck with a ridiculous story yesterday in the face of all evidence. As he clung to it, he blew his chance to help his brothers out.

And now he's going to have to reap that whirlwind.

"How did you sleep?" I ask politely.

He looks like hell. I needn't have asked.

"I did not sleep. I couldn't."

"Sorry to hear that. Maybe if you do the right thing, you'll be able to sleep tonight."

Silence. We wait. He chooses not to answer.

"Have you thought about what I said yesterday?"

"Yes. That is all I could think about. That and my mother." His voice cracks when he mentions his mother.

"Well?"

He looks me in the eyes. I see a scared human, exhausted and desperate. I feel uneasy. If it is an act, it is an Oscar-winning one.

"I will tell you anything you want to know. I will tell you only the truth."

"Excellent."

"Tell me about the car."

He intakes a long breath, then lets it out slowly. Here it comes. He's going to tell the truth.

"The car did not move."

You've got to be kidding me.

I'm indignant.

"How can you look me in the face and lie to me?" I demand.

He looks cowed. "My car never moved. It didn't. I swear it didn't."

"Bullshit!" I erupt, my anger genuine. I can't contain it. "I showed you the pictures! We have a video!"

"That is not possible. Please," he entreats, "I tell you the truth."

I scoot my chair forward. He recoils at my approach, but I just reach to him and pull the two photos out of his breast pocket. He looks wary, as if his head is filling with visions of Abu Ghraib.

"Okay, Yusif," I begin, "My boss is furious that you will not tell the truth. Yesterday, I offered you a chance to get your brothers back home to your mother. Today, he won't allow me to do that. You had that chance and you threw it away by lying to me."

I pause. Mustafa translates. Yusif looks stricken.

"Today, I can only offer you this deal. You tell us the truth and my boss says he will release one of your brothers. Only one. This deal ends today. If you don't take it, your mother might be alone for a long time."

The color drains from Yusif's face. His eyes start to water.

I scoot my chair a little closer. Now our knees are a cat's whisker from touching. My face is inches from his. I hand him the photos of his brothers and order, "Hold these." He takes them, and I see him sneak a glance down at them.

"Go ahead, look at them." He does.

"Now, which one will you save?"

Mustafa's translation hits him like a sneaker wave, and he stares at his brothers like a man being dragged out to sea. He knows there will be no rescue.

His eyes meet mine. Pleading, he cries, "I can't. Don't make me choose."

"You must. I gave you a chance yesterday."

He starts to hyperventilate. His breathing is shallow, fast, and ragged.

"Please, I beg you. Please don't make me do this."

"Your mother will be alone."

"No!"

"Who goes home to her, Yusif?"

A sob escapes him. Tears spill down his face and splatter on the concrete floor. He drops his head almost into his knees. I back up to give him some space. He clutches the photos as he gasps.

"Please. Please. Please. I am telling the truth. I cannot choose."

His sobbing grows uncontrollable. "No. No. Don't make me do this . . ." He gasps for breath and rocks back and forth, clutching his sides. One of the photos flutters to the floor. I reach for it and put it back in his hand and then remain standing in front of him.

"Which one, Yusif? Who will you save?"

No answer. More sobbing.

I lean over at the waist and put my face close to his.

"My boss is firm on this, Yusif. Tomorrow I won't be able to help any of you. You've got to give me something. I want to help you."

Through the sobs, he wails, "The car didn't move!"

I walk away and kick my chair onto its side.

"You're killing me Yusif! Don't just sit there and lie to me! That won't save anybody! Come on, for God's sake, if you're going to lie, make up a better story! Tell me it was stolen!"

"It wasn't!"

"Anything, for the sake of your mother, Yusif. Come on! Tell me your neighbor has the same car! Give me something!"

Suddenly Yusif grows still. A sob catches in his throat. He looks up at me again for the first time in minutes.

"That's it!" He exclaims. The fear in his red-rimmed eyes evaporates. He looks . . . almost excited.

"What do you mean?"

"My neighbor! My neighbor!"

"What are you talking about Yusif?"

"Three houses down on the right. He has the same car I have!"

"You expect me to believe that?

"Yes! It is true. His name is Muhammad. He's twenty-two. Black hair. Glasses. He's a troublemaker in our neighborhood."

"And he owns a BMW?"

Yusif sees a lifeline. "Yes, yes! A blue 325, just like mine."

"Why can't I see it in this photograph then?" I say holding up the still image the helicopter shot at the apartment complex.

"He parks it in a carport. You wouldn't see it from the air."

I study him intently. Five seconds pass. Ten.

Could this be true?

Fifteen seconds pass. He looks utterly sincere. Nobody could act this well. I'm going to have to check this out.

I pick up my chair and set it upright.

"Yusif. I will return in a few minutes. I am going to ask your brothers about this neighbor. But if I find out you are lying . . ."

I leave it at that. I slip out the door and walk down the hall to Steve's booth. He's interrogating the middle brother. A tap on the door prompts Steve to open it. He steps into the hall. "What's up?"

"Hey, just for shits and giggles, can you find out a little bit about the neighbor three houses down on the right? I need a description and the kind of car he drives."

"Sure." He steps back inside. I dash to the Hollywood room and tune in. Steve starts off by asking the brother to describe all the families living around their apartment. Using another copy of the still photo taken by the helicopter, the brother populates the neighborhood for us. When he gets to the third house on the right, the brother says, "That's Muhammad's house. He's twenty-two years old."

"What sort of car does he drive?"

"He has a blue BMW 325. Just like my brother Yusif's."

What have I done?

Guilt stabs me. The image of Yusif doubled over in the booth, blooms in my mind. I psychologically savaged him.

I run to the 'gator pit and find Cliff. I've got to be sure. "Hey, you know that chopper that followed our guys?"

"Sure."

"Did the pilots have eyes on it the entire time?"

"I don't know. I think so, but I haven't seen the entire video. They just sent over the stills."

"Can you find out?"

"Yeah, let me make a phone call."

I wait anxiously by my desk as Cliff disappears. When he returns he says, "The pilot just told me they briefly lost the car in traffic, then found it again in front of the apartment."

I feel like somebody's just stabbed me in the heart.

"Cliff, we have the wrong guys."

Yusif and his brothers had nothing to do with this. He's been telling the truth, and I presumed him to be a liar. Instead of keeping an open mind, I judged him to be just as guilty as the others.

I go to tell Randy what's happened. The fact that Yusif does freelance work for a network worries him. He calls the task force leadership on the phone and they fret over the possible media implications of what's just happened. They see it as a civil affairs problem. We've been interrogating an innocent journalist.

Randy muses, "If he's pissed off enough, he could really give us a black eye."

All of that is true. But I just see Yusif, spent and broken, pleading for me not to make him chose between his brothers.

Cliff appears and passes along some news. A conventional unit just raided Muhammad's house. They didn't find the bodies, but there was a weapon's cache concealed inside the home and a blue BMW 325 in the carport. He was the guilty one after all.

A civil affairs captain arrives. She intends to sit down with all three brothers, apologize, and offer them compensation.

"No," I say, "I will sit down with Yusif. I did this to him. I have to make it right."

The walk back to the booth is the longest of my life. What can I say?

I enter silently. Yusif has composed himself. Mustafa gives me a blank look. I sit down in front of Yusif, but I push my chair back, giving him back his space.

"Yusif. You are telling the truth."

Relief floods his expression. "Yes."

"I have no words. There are no words to tell you how sorry I am. I was wrong. I don't even know where to begin."

Mustafa translates. Yusif listens quietly.

"I owe you a profound apology. I have wronged you."

I'm not sure how to go on. I'm the one near tears now. I

make a fist and thump it against my heart twice in an Iraqi gesture of sincerity.

Yusif says, "Mister Matthew, don't be upset. You have a very difficult job. You are doing what is best for Iraq. There is no need to apologize."

Is he sincere? Is he running an approach on me? I can't tell anymore. I've been here not yet even two months, and the paranoia and suspicion I've had to hone in the booth has jaded me to basic human interaction.

"It's not fair, Yusif, what you've gone through. It's not fair."

"If it makes my country a better place, so be it."

I look in his face, and for the first time in my career, I'm absolutely certain I'm listening to honest words.

"I'm sorry, Yusif. I'm so sorry."

I look in his eyes. I see forgiveness. And that is the hardest thing for me to accept.

PART III
GOING IN CIRCLES

Every knot has someone to undo it.

—ARAB PROVERB

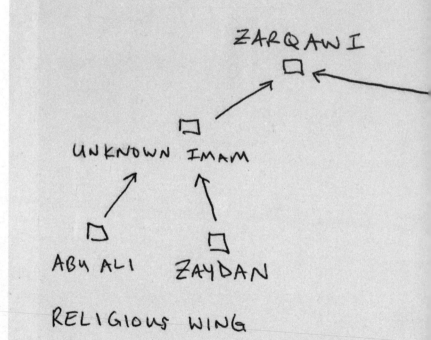

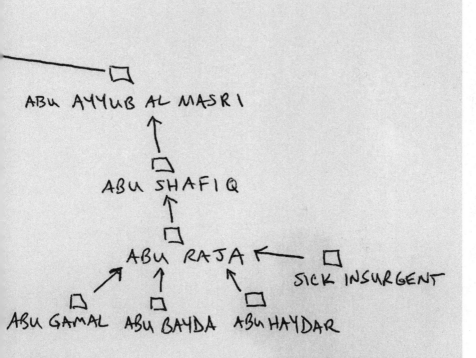

ABU AYYUB AL MASRI

ABU SHAFIQ

ABU RAJA ← SICK INSURGENT

ABU GAMAL   ABU BAYDA   ABU HAYDAR

OPERATIONAL WING

Fifteen

CAT AND MOUSE

I T'S A NEW day, and I'm trying to put Yusif behind me, but it's difficult. I've promised myself that when I go back into the booth, I will remember my sense of humanity and compassion. I don't want to end up like some of our veterans here, bloated with hate for our enemy.

The hunt for Zarqawi has hit a brick wall. We can't find Abu Shafiq, and without another rung on the ladder, we're condemned to spin in circles.

I'll be watching two important interrogations this afternoon. Mary is slated to interrogate Abu Haydar. We're all puzzled about him. Is he just the cameraman? If that's the case, he's the low man in the group's hierarchy, maybe even lower than Abu Gamal. Yet he carries himself with such assurance.

In another booth, Steve will interrogate Abu Raja, the only one talking at this point. Even a fragment from him might help us solve enough of the puzzle to reveal the group's leader and allow us to focus our search.

In the Hollywood room, I tune into Mary first. She sits down with Abu Haydar, who looks stonily at her. The coldness between them is palpable even through the monitor. They speak in English.

"Did you get enough sleep?" Mary asks.

"Yes, I slept fine," Abu Haydar says in British-accented English. He's a bulky man with dark hair and an aquiline nose that dominates his face. He somehow manages to look dignified even though he is squeezed into his orange jumpsuit.

"Have you thought anymore about our talk yesterday?" Mary asks.

Abu Haydar sits ramrod straight in his plastic chair. He's so calm that I wonder if his heart rate has even hit sixty beats a minute. "Yes, I did actually, and my answer has not changed." He acts like he could be having a discussion with a recalcitrant student. Mary doesn't seem to detect his tone.

"So you maintain that you were only at the house as a cameraman?"

"Yes. Abu Raja told me to bring a camera."

He gives Mary a slight grin. He looks like a child who just got away with something naughty. As he waits for her response, he absently strokes his beard. His hands are massive.

"That's just not believable, Abu Haydar," Mary says.

"Nevertheless, it is the truth."

Mary decides to take another path. "You just got out of Abu Ghraib four months ago. Why would you risk going to a house with suicide bombers?"

"Exactly!" Abu Haydar exclaims, as if his student has just tumbled to the correct answer to a problem. "Who would do such a thing? Certainly not me. If I had known there were suicide bombers there, I wouldn't have gone to the house." He flashes another grin.

Mary studies her notes and avoids his gaze, allowing Abu Haydar to dominate the discussion. His eyes never leave her face. Mary plays with her pen, tapping on the side of her notepad as she thinks through her next move.

"Look, Abu Raja has already admitted he knew there were suicide bombers at the house."

Actually, he hasn't, not yet anyway, but that's a good move. Mary's running the We Know All approach on him.

She continues, "We know that Abu Raja arranged the meeting. We also know that Abu Gamal wired the suicide vests."

Abu Haydar's smile remains undimmed. He sits politely and seems totally unfazed by what he's just heard.

"It isn't hard to figure out that you were there to video-tape their last rites."

Abu Haydar measures his words. He starts with, "Per-haps . . . but the truth is I didn't know that before I arrived."

"What do you mean?"

"I was just as shocked as you would have been when I walked into that house and saw those foreigners there. I'd been asked to videotape a wedding."

"Wait," Mary asks, unable to conceal a note of excitement, "how did you know they were foreigners?"

Abu Haydar sighs. The student has asked a foolish ques-tion, but all must be answered no matter how silly. "Would you not know the difference between Americans and Europeans?" He frames his answer with a condescending smile that Mary either misses or chooses to ignore. As he waits for her response, he strokes his beard again.

"Where were these foreigners from?"

"I did not ask them. I did not have time. We had just arrived when your helicopters showed up."

Mary retreats to her notebook. She scribbles something, then, without looking up, she changes gears again. "You know you won't be here much longer, right?"

Abu Haydar offers no response.

"You won't have many more chances to cooperate."

She lets that sink in. Abu Haydar appears unconcerned. He stops stroking his beard and places his hand back in his lap. He looks very proper and well mannered.

"They're going to transfer you to Abu Ghraib."

Mary's trying to intimidate him. But he's much too smart for that. He sits unblinking, his eyes fixed on her head.

She looks up at him. "Do you want to go back to Abu Ghraib? Do you really want to risk the court again? You were released on a two-to-one vote. Do you think the judges will be so lenient next time?"

Abu Haydar lets out a long sigh. One hand comes up from his lap, palm out, in a gesture of openness. "Young lady, I will simply be forced to tell them the same thing I've told you. Abu Raja asked me to bring a camera and film a wedding. That's all."

Mary gets angry, "Who's going to believe that ridiculous story?"

"Do you have a better one?" Abu Haydar counters.

"Sure. How about this: Abu Raja asked you to go with

him to videotape suicide bombers before they went on their mission. You knew they were going to be there."

"And you have this on film?" Abu Haydar asks. It is the sly question of a defense attorney. He asks the question because he knows the answer.

Mary glowers at him. "There was nothing on the tape," she admits.

"Then it is not a better story," he dismisses it with a wave of his hand.

No, he's not dismissing her version. He just dismissed her.

Abu Haydar knows our system because he went through it four months ago. Knowing that Mary can't touch him, he exudes confidence. I bet he could beat the rap, too. There's no evidence to counter his story, save common sense.

"Fine," Mary spits at him. She's clearly infuriated and frustrated. "You can go back to your cell and think about your upcoming court date at Abu Ghraib. I hope the judges are as sympathetic as last time. Put on your mask."

Abu Haydar slowly reaches to the floor and picks up his mask. As he pulls it over his face, I see his devilish grin disappear under the black cloth.

Sixteen

THE LEADER

"A RE YOU READY?" I ask Steve. We're in the 'gator pit finishing the pregame warm-up for Abu Raja. Behind us, Mary's typing away at her computer, fuming over what just happened in the booth.

Steve looks over at Cliff.

"Yeah. I think we've got a good plan. Let's go give it a shot."

"Good luck," Cliff tells him, shooting nasal spray into his nose.

Steve heads off to get Abu Raja. Before I leave for the Hollywood room, Cliff asks me, "Did you hear what happened to Bobby the other night?"

My heart stops.

"No."

"He went out with a raid team up north."

"Okay. That's what he's supposed to be doing."

Bobby's at an outstation, carrying out field interrogations.

When a raid team hits a house, whoever is inside is questioned on the spot by Bobby and an interpreter. He'll be doing this until June—unless he gets hurt or killed. This SF team lost two members to a suicide bomber the month we arrived.

Cliff rubs his nose absently. "Well, the raid team approaches their target house. A twelve-year-old boy bursts through a door on the balcony holding an AK. A sniper shot him dead."

"Holy shit."

"Turns out the kid thought our guys were a Shia death squad coming for his family. He was trying to defend his parents."

He lets that sink in. I feel a twist of guilt thinking of Yusif and the cost of this war to the civilian population.

"You want to know what the real kick in the gut was?"

"God, Cliff, just tell me."

He looks slightly wounded, but gives it up anyway. "It turned out to be the wrong house."

It's horrible news. Intelligence is never perfect, and who knows how that house came to be targeted. It's another reason why it's so important that we are right when we get our information.

"That's a tragedy," I manage.

"Yeah. Thought you should know." Cliff turns and heads back to his desk in the analyst's pit.

"Thanks," I say to his back. He waves a hand in response.

I hurry to the Hollywood room, notepad in hand. I arrive just as Abu Raja enters Steve's interrogation booth. The guard sits him down, and Abu Raja removes his mask.

Steve asks about Abu Raja's health, and the two exchange pleasantries. The interrogation flows from there. Steve puts a little more pressure on him. Abu Raja is not a strong man. He starts talking.

At one point, Steve revisits the farmhouse. "So tell me something, Abu Raja."

"Yes, sir. What would you like to know?"

"I want to know why you were at the house."

"I was at the house on orders from Abu Shafiq."

"Did you know why you were going there?"

"No."

"There were five of you in the car. Abu Gamal drove, right?"

"Yes."

"Abu Haydar had the video camera."

"Yes."

"Was Abu Bayda the leader of your group, then?"

"No. I do not know why he was there."

"Who put the whole group together?"

Abu Raja doesn't answer at first. Instead, he looks up, directly into the camera. His face is a mask of despair. This is a man who cannot handle prison. A week here, and he's already haggard and gaunt. Broken. I sympathize with him. How many pediatricians come to this pass? Those who make desperate choices.

"Abu Raja, come on. Who put the group together?"

He lets out a long sigh. His chin falls to his chest. "I did."

I sit straight up.

"So on orders from your boss, Abu Shafiq, you gathered

Abu Haydar, your wife's cousin Abu Gamal, and Abu Bayda?"

"Yes."

"How did you know Abu Bayda?"

"I didn't. Abu Shafiq knew him."

Steve pummels Abu Raja with more questions, but Abu Raja won't give up anything else today, and Steve finally ends it. A guard escorts Abu Raja back to his cell. Steve and I meet with Cliff in the 'gator pit.

"Abu Raja just admitted again that he was the leader of the Group of Five," Steve says.

"Seriously?" Cliff says.

"Yes."

"What do you think, Matthew?"

"I don't know if I buy it."

Steve considers that. "You know, I'm not sure I believe him either. Maybe he's trying to cover for the real leader."

"What? Why?" asks Cliff.

"For one thing," Steve says, "he's too much of a puss. The guy is a weak link."

"Exactly," I add. "He doesn't act like a leader."

"What do you mean?" Cliff asks.

"He doesn't have the right aura," Steve replies.

"Steve's right," I add, "Abu Raja is not an impressive man. He's very smart, but he doesn't exude confidence."

"Could it be an act?"

Steve and I look at each other. Is Abu Raja running an approach on us? Is he purposely acting like a broken momma's boy?

"Could be?" I say with a shrug.

Steve shakes his head, "I don't think so, guys. Look at Abu Bayda. He's much older, and he's supposedly an imam, right?"

"Right," Cliff confirms.

"Well, maybe he's trying to protect Abu Bayda."

"Yeah," I say, "I think you're right."

"Write it up. Could be he's telling the truth," Cliff suggests.

Wheels within wheels are at play here. Even this break is suspect. If only we could get a little more from Abu Raja, maybe push him to reveal whether or not he's running an approach on us. ████████████████████████████████ ██ ██ ████████████████████████████ Randy will soon want to make way for the next wave of prisoners.

Seventeen

FAULT LINES

I

T'S AWKWARD TO be the new guy and the senior interrogator. I'm meant to assign 'gators to detainees, but
Randy has made it clear to me that Mary is to interrogate our top priorities whether I think she's suitable or not. I
have to approve every ruse or a trick in the booth and monitor the interrogations to make sure we're in compliance with
both the Geneva Conventions and the Department of Defense regulations. It's my job to give advice on interrogation
strategies. But the old-schoolers haven't accepted the new
methods.

One morning I hit my table right after ten o'clock. Ann
comes by to chat. It's been lonely without Bobby, and seeing
her cheers me up.

"How'd it go with the remains of the Group of Five last
night?" I ask. We still have Abu Haydar, Abu Raja, and Abu
Bayda in the prison.

"Nathan had some luck with Abu Raja. The other two

aren't talking. Lenny's been working Abu Bayda hard with the You're Totally Screwed routine."

"I wish they'd come around."

"I don't think that will happen. Take a look."

Across the 'gator pit, I see the conference room filling up an hour before our eleven o'clock meeting.

"What's going on?"

Ann shrugs. I get up to go check it out. As I get to the door, I stop an analyst and ask, "What's up?"

The analyst looks distinctly uncomfortable. Something is afoot. "Uh, we're just, um, going to discuss Abu Bayda."

That's interesting. The senior interrogator should have been invited.

I slip into the room and take a seat at the back. Mary walks in. So do Tom and an ████████████████████████ analyst named Edith, Cliff's counterpart on the night shift. Though none of them look at me, I'm the two-ton elephant in the room. It becomes obvious that they deliberately excluded me from this meeting.

Everyone here is an old-schooler and an Iraq veteran. Most have been in country for a year. I resolve to stay quiet and listen.

Mary starts things off. "Okay, we know Abu Bayda has to be somebody important, right?"

Tom agrees. "Yeah. You can tell by his mannerisms that he's the leader of the group."

Heads nod all around. Edith adds, "He's a player, alright. He's definitely got a lot of power."

Mary says, "He's a lot older than the others. And he's an imam."

More nods.

"So far, we haven't gotten anything out of him," says Tom.

"Nothing," Mary echoes. "How do we get him talking?"

Lenny is quick to offer his two cents, "Listen, we just need to get him to understand that his fate is in our hands. We control him. If he doesn't talk, he's going to swing."

Mary agrees. "Yeah. He's not getting out of here without our help."

Edith chimes in, "He's arrogant, right?"

Tom, Mary, and Lenny nod. Edith continues, "Look, he thinks he's powerful. But actually, now he's powerless. You need to break him down until he realizes he's got no power, no influence."

"Right," Lenny says, "Tear down his self-respect. That should level the playing field."

I can't believe I'm hearing this. If you tried to crush an American colonel's sense of self with words alone, would it work?

I stay silent.

The conversation continues. All the old-school buzz-words are tossed around. The more I hear, the more agitated I become. Randy has set Abu Bayda as our top priority, followed by Abu Haydar and Abu Raja. Mary, Tom, and Lenny have been interrogating Abu Haydar and Abu Bayda. They've never built rapport with these guys, gotten to know them as people, or earned their trust. Why do they think any of their strategies are going to work? You can't get to home plate if you've never rounded first base.

A lull falls over the meeting. I can't help myself. I hear myself ask, "Hey, does Abu Bayda have any kids?"

Edith actually laughs. Another person guffaws. Lenny looks pissed, and Mary refuses to acknowledge me. Edith chooses to respond. With a *you're the new guy so I'm going to give you the 411* tone in her voice, she lectures me: "He'll never fall for that. When he joined Al Qaida he wrote off his family. They all do."

Mary mirrors Edith's tone. "Yeah. Once they join up, they've got no loyalty to their family—only to Al Qaida."

More snickering. I feel humiliated. Could I be this far off the mark?

Abu Ali.

Have I misread what's going on here so badly?

Zaydan.

I may be the new guy, but haven't I proven myself?

Abu Gamal.

No. The fleeting self-doubt evaporates. I know I'm right on this one.

The hostility in the room is palpable now. I am the senior interrogator, but this clique doesn't respect me or my opinions. Should I confront them? Should I lay the evidence on the table? Should I remind them of the breaks we've made these past three weeks with Love of Family approaches? With earned trust and respect?

No. They are convinced their methods of fear and control are the only way to win in the booth.

Should I point out that nothing is more important in Arab culture than family? Their family bonds are far stronger than ours, and no Iraqi would give up his family.

No. They don't care about Arab culture.

Should I point out that true Kool-Aid-drinking Al Qaida believers are exceptionally rare? Are they blind to the nuances of this war? I've read that most Senators and Congressmen back home do not understand the Shia-Sunni split in Iraq. Our ignorance of our enemy after three years of fighting astonishes me.

For most of our detainees, Al Qaida is an expedient, nothing more. The organization reached out to Sunnis at a moment of great crisis, and many Sunnis felt they had no choice but to accept their aid. Some of our detainees have had moral qualms about Al Qaida. Few of them espouse the Al Qaida ideology or believe in it.

I want to look around the room and say, "Iraqis are not jihadists. We can't fit them into one category. Not every Iraqi sells out his family when he joins Al Qaida."

I start to say it, but then stop. Apart from Tom, nobody here has any interest in the new techniques. This generation of interrogators was deeply steeped in the force-on-force mentality back home, in their previous tours here in Iraq, Afghanistan, and Guantánamo.

Instead of adding to the growing rift, I get up and leave the room. I'll let what happens in the booth speak for itself.

Had they been amenable, I would have suggested the opposite approach. Instead of trying to crush Abu Bayda's self-importance, why not use rapport to build him up and then earn his respect by demonstrating a knowledge of his culture and religion and even sympathy towards his cause?

I return to the 'gator pit struggling with my emotions. As a leader, I can't let them influence my decisions, but I can't help but feel infuriated. I'm angry, not with the way they treated me but with their unwillingness to listen to new ideas. Change does not come easy.

At eleven o'clock, we gather in the conference room.

Those in the previous meeting studiously avoid me. I can sense that if I don't figure out a way to manage this schism, it will damage our efforts.

Randy comes in and puts his foot up on a chair. "Listen up. I know you all are working as hard as you can. We've made some good progress in the past few days. But the pressure is on us to deliver. President Bush called the task force commander again. General Casey is coming personally to check on us. We've got to work our way up the ladder."

He pauses, then changes gears, "Okay, let's see where we stand."

A photo of Abu Bayda's face appears on the wall.

"Lenny?"

Lenny stands and gives a short summary of his interrogations with Abu Bayda.

"He hasn't given up anything so far."

Randy asks, "What's your recommendation?"

Lenny pauses. "Retain and exploit."

Randy looks to Cliff for an analyst opinion, and Cliff nods in approval.

"Agreed. Next. Abu Haydar." His face appears on the wall.

Lenny remains standing and says, "He still claims he was in the house to film a wedding."

Randy's face grows more strained as he listens. Lenny's been working Abu Haydar for over a week without any results.

Lenny looks uncertain when Randy asks for his recommendation. "He's not working us up the ladder. Transfer to Abu Ghraib," he finally replies. This leaves the recommendation up to the detainee's analyst.

Randy turns to Cliff. "Well?"

"I agree, he's not giving us anything that Abu Raja can't give us."

"Negative," Randy says. "He's staying. Moving on. Abu Raja."

His photo hits the wall.

Nathan stands. So far, I've been very impressed with Nathan. He's a mature 'gator, he served in the army. He retired a few years ago and started his own business in Utah. A family man with several kids, he's in Iraq as a civilian contractor and he's proven to be flexible and creative. Together, Nathan and Steve have made significant progress on Abu Raja.

Nathan summarizes, "Abu Raja is talking. Once we got past the wedding story, anyway. He's told us that his boss is Abu Shafiq. Abu Shafiq told him to get Abu Haydar and bring him to the farmhouse with a video camera."

Randy asks, "What about locations on Abu Shafiq?"

"Same as before. He said he meets him at a falafel stand in Baghdad or at a mosque in Mansur district."

Steve chimes in, "He still denies knowing that there would be suicide bombers in the house. He says that Abu Shafiq just told him where to go, not what to expect there."

"Anything else?" Randy asks.

"That's it," Nathan says. "Recommend retain and exploit."

Again Randy looks at Cliff, and Cliff nods in agreement.

"Okay. Abu Raja stays," Randy finishes.

The meeting continues. We go through all the current detainees. After we finish and I make the assignments for the day, I walk back to Randy's office.

"I'd like to try something new," I begin.

Randy appears interested, "Okay, what've you got?"

"I'd like to switch up interrogators on Abu Haydar and Abu Bayda."

A torn expression crosses his face. My request has struck a nerve. "Won't happen. Sorry. My hands are tied."

What is going on here?

"There's no way?"

"Zero. None. Don't ask again."

"Okay, then. Thanks."

I leave Randy's office thoroughly disappointed. It is the primary role of the senior interrogator to assign detainees to 'gators. Somebody above Randy is micromanaging us.

When I return to the 'gator pit, Ann's left. Steve is busy going over the details of the next pass at Abu Raja with Cliff. Mary's huddled with Edith. Today she's scheduled to interrogate both Abu Bayda and Abu Haydar.

I find my chair and start going through some paperwork. My intuition tells me that the Group of Five holds the key. If we can just get the right approach, we may just find that next rung up the ladder. I pull out a notebook and study it. Since I arrived, I've been updating a wire diagram that shows the connections between our detainees. Right now, we have too many empty boxes and too big a gap between our detainees and Zarqawi, who's name sits at the top of the diagram. He's at least one or two steps on the ladder above the others.

Where do Abu Bayda, Abu Raja, and Abu Haydar fit in? And who is this Abu Shafiq? Nobody else has mentioned him. Did Abu Raja invent that name, or is he a missing rung on our ladder? If so, which wing: religious or operational?

I don't know. But we're running out of time. Every morning, the news brings fresh waves of terror from Baghdad.

Bodies turn up every sunrise, bound with bullet wounds in their heads. Most show signs of torture. Shia death squads wreak havoc with kidnappings and random murders. The Sunnis send suicide bombers into Shia marketplaces. The country is spiraling out of control.

Eighteen

THE EYES OF FATIMA

MID-APRIL 2006

SOMETIMES, SOMETHING HAPPENS that injects in me a little hope for the future of Iraq. We receive a valuable tip from a concerned citizen who alerts us to the presence of an Al Qaida operative at a downtown Baghdad Internet café. A raid team charges out of the compound. In minutes, they've nailed a scrawny, curly-haired college kid and they bring him back to the compound.

Iraq needs more concerned citizens.

When our Al Qaida college kid reaches the compound, I assign Marcia to the interrogation. She's an army NCO, Hispanic in origin but could easily pass as an Arab with her long dark hair and big soulful eyes. Arabs would call them "the eyes of Fatima," the daughter of the Prophet, which is one of the most flattering compliments a woman can receive in the Islamic world. In the booth, Marcia puts them to good use. They give her an earnest, trustworthy quality, allowing her to build a unique rapport with her detainees.

When I took over from David as senior interrogator, he warned me that Marcia was a high-maintenance interrogator, meaning she needed watching. She was accused once of bringing a detainee into an interrogation booth for no reason other than wanting to smoke in the air conditioning, since the only time interrogators could smoke inside the building and not outside in the desert heat was if their detainee smoked with them in the booth. I didn't know if the story was true, but with me, everyone started with a clean slate. What I know is that while she's not an old-schooler, she does conduct her interrogations by the book. She uses the approaches well, but they only take her so far.

Over the course of four days, I watch her work on Ismail, the Al Qaida computer geek. She develops an excellent rapport with him, partly because they're both young but also because they're both smokers and Marcia never fails to give him a cigarette. By day two, they're sitting in the booth, smoking and talking like old friends.

But such good rapport can become a burden if not used correctly. Marcia finds it difficult to ratchet up the intensity of the interrogation. She can't escalate the tension without destroying the rapport they've built. She starts going in circles.

The answer to the problem is guilt. Guilt-trip the newfound friend into giving up information. Marcia eventually intuits this and pushes hard on this front. Time after time, I see her from the Hollywood room telling Ismail, "I'm your friend, right? I give you cigarettes. I make sure you're well treated, right? Now it's your turn to help me."

Ismail's patented response: "I wish I could, but I don't know anything."

He was caught with DVDs of insurgent point-of-view attacks on American forces, beheading videos, and Al Qaida propaganda films. The Sergeant Schultz defense doesn't cut it.

One morning, I arrive in the 'gator pit to find Marcia waiting for me. "What do you think of today's Randyism?" she asks me. I look over at the whiteboard and laugh as I read aloud, "Little boys check under their beds at night for the bogeyman. The bogeyman checks under his bed for Randy."

"What do you think I can do better with Ismail? I've tried everything I can think of, Love of Family, Love of Comrades, We Know All . . . I even suggested we could pay him off. Nothing's working."

We walk over to my table as I think about this. "Well, he's pretty young. He's scared. Maybe we should try a Boss Introduction."

Marcia lights up at that. "That's what I was thinking."

If you've ever bought a car at a dealership, then you've probably been a victim of the boss introduction. When the negotiation stalls, the salesman calls in his boss, a person with social prestige, to pressure you. This method works even better against Arabs since their culture is strongly hierarchical.

After our 11 A.M. meeting, Marcia goes into one of the interrogation booths and meets with Ismail while I watch from the Hollywood room.

"Ismail, I like you," she begins. Ismail speaks perfect English.

"I like you, too. You have been very kind to me."

Ismail sits hunched up within himself. His hands shake

constantly. He has perpetual jitters. Even in their most re-laxed moments together, Ismail is never far from the realiza-tion that he's bound for Abu Ghraib.

Marcia's eyes of Fatima radiate compassion. They don't calm him down, but they do rivet his attention. She smiles warmly, "Look, you're a good person who got trapped. I un-derstand that. That's why I've asked my boss to come meet you today."

"Your boss?" Ismail asks hesitantly.

"Yes. My boss is the type of person you want on your side. He can influence people with just a few phone calls. He can speak to the judges on your behalf."

Ismail's eyes go wide. Marcia's offered him a lifeline, and he suddenly sees hope.

"Really? He can help me?"

"Yes. He doesn't talk to many detainees, I'll tell you that right now. And I'm taking a risk by asking him to talk to you."

"Risk?"

"Yes. I'm taking a chance on you Ismail. If it doesn't work out, it'll damage my reputation here. I like my job, and I want to keep it."

"I won't do anything that gets you in trouble," he prom-ises.

"Thank you. Just know that this is a very rare chance. I'm counting on you, okay? Don't make me look bad."

"No, no, don't worry."

"I trust you, Ismail. I really do."

That's my cue. I leave the Hollywood room and hustle down to the interrogation booth. As I walk, I turn myself into the hard-nosed, aloof boss who is skeptical but willing to give Ismail a chance. I must exude authority. This is the metamorphosis of the old techniques—blending them with our knowledge of Arab culture, similar to Tom and Steve's routine a few weeks before. I stop at a garbage can in the hallway and grab a piece of scrap paper for my clipboard.

Marcia lets me in and introduces me.

I sit down next to the table in the room with the clipboard in my lap, its front hidden from Ismail. Marcia sits on the other side of the table and Ismail sits alone in front of us. I look down at my clipboard and produce a pen.

"Okay, I need to ask you some questions," I say.

Ismail looks thoroughly intimidated. He manages a nod.

I want to keep him on edge without overdoing it. He already sees me as his lifeline.

"Ismail, before the war began, you were going to college, is that right?"

"Yes. I studied computers at Baghdad University."

I pretend to check something off on my clipboard. He watches me intently. I continue, "Why did you leave school?"

"My father. Well, he died. I had to move back in with my mother and take care of her. But I could not find much work."

I pretend to check another box. Then I look up over my clipboard at him. "How did your father die?"

Ismail looks mortified. "It is too painful to discuss."

This is a perfect chance to build rapport.

"I understand."

He looks relieved. That was a major sore point with Marcia. She couldn't find out what happened to his father either. I wonder if he was killed by a Shia militia.

"How did you end up working for Al Qaida?"

Ismail gets defensive. "I . . . I did not know who I was working for. I just went to the mosque one day looking for work. This man offered me a job. I didn't think I was doing anything wrong. I just edited the videos he gave me, adding graphics and verses from the Koran."

"What did you do with them when you were finished?"

"I posted them on Web sites I had built for him. Then I gave the finished videos back to him on DVDs."

"What was on these DVDs?"

Ismail is suddenly still. Over the past four days he's been a bundle of jitters, so the transformation is stark. His hands stop shaking. He quits fidgeting. He looks me in the eyes. "Horrible things. But I did not have anything to do with them."

Horrible things—he's right about that. Beheadings. Executions. I wonder if he edited the final versions of the two videos Bobby showed me.

"What happened to these DVDs after you gave them to your boss at the mosque?"

Ismail shrugs. "I'm not sure. Maybe they were copied and sold on the street."

Al Qaida propaganda.

I don't say anything to this. Instead, I frown and check a box. The frown elicits a sharp intake of breath. I glance up. Ismail's riveted.

I set the clipboard upside down on the table. Then I pick up my chair and move it right in front of his. I sit down, our knees almost touching. I pretend to study him. The silence unnerves him. His hands start to shake again. He vibrates with nervousness. He knows the penalty for working with Al Qaida. I am his way to cheat the hangman's noose.

The silence continues. I look him over again. He's sitting ramrod straight, shoulders back, head erect. All week long he's been so scrunched up inside himself that I haven't been able to get a sense of how tall he is. Now I can see he's about five seven, with maybe an extra two inches of mop-top curly black hair thrown in for good measure.

I bring my hand up to my chin and start scratching at my patchwork beard, as if lost in thought.

"All right, Ismail," I say slowly, "I'm going to trust you."

His hands stop shaking. Relief washes over him. "Thank you, sir. Thank you."

"I don't do this often, but Marcia told me you are a special case. I believe her, and I believe you. You needed a job, Al Qaida gave you one. You were just looking for a way to take care of your mother and get back to school someday."

"Yes. Yes, sir, that's true."

"I'm going to offer you something. It is a one-time offer. You can take it or not, but if not, it will never be offered again."

"Yes, sir."

He is extremely deferential to me. With Marcia, he's much more friendly and informal. He's right where we need him to be.

"I can make some phone calls. I can make sure that when you leave this place you will be taken care of and your case will be viewed very favorably."

"Thank you, sir."

"I will do this on one condition."

"Condition, sir? What condition?" He asks uncertainly.

"You have to tell me who you worked for."

Ismail goes rigid. Not a muscle twitches. He doesn't even blink and he seems to be holding his breath.

I hold his gaze. Seconds pass.

This is the crossroads of his life. He must give up his boss to save his own life. Will he do it? It is the ultimate test. What sort of man are you, Ismail? Will you save yourself?

He glances over at Marcia, whose eyes and smile project encouragement. He looks back at me.

"I worked for a guy in the mosque. I didn't know his name," he finally answers. His words lack conviction. This is his last line of defense, but I can tell he's got no stomach left for the consequences.

I decide to give him one final chance. Let this last stand crumble.

"Ismail," I ratchet up the authority in my voice. I'm polite and professional, but now I try to convey the finality of what is about to happen. "No. That's not good enough. If you want this deal, you have to tell me his name. This is your last chance."

Ismail turns to Marcia and searches for solace in her eyes of Fatima. He finds in them trust and security.

He takes a long breath and releases it. Then he whispers, "Abu Raja."

The leader of the Group of Five.

My face remains a mask. I give nothing away, but inside I'm reeling from this revelation and its implications.

"Abu Raja? That's who you worked for? He's the man you met at the mosque?"

"Yes."

"So what does Abu Raja do?"

Ismail answers, "I don't know exactly. But he's the one who brought me the videos. I edited them and gave them back."

"What does he look like?"

"Bald on top. Mustache. He wears glasses. He's a doctor."

That's our man. And now we know he's one of Al Qaida's public affairs officers.

I won't reveal the fact that we already have him in custody. In fact, I'll lead Ismail to believe we're going to go looking for him.

"Where can we find Abu Raja?"

"At the mosque in Baghdad. The largest one in the Mansur neighborhood."

"Thank you, Ismail. I'll make sure you're taken care of when you leave here. For now, we'll bring you an extra meal and pillow."

"Thank you, sir."

"I'm going to go make some phone calls. I need you to continue to work with Marcia. I'll be watching."

I stand and turn for the door.

Before he leaves our base, I'll be sure there's a note in his file explaining just how helpful he's been. The judges will look favorably at that, and if he's lucky, he'll get only five years instead of twenty or worse. Nonetheless, five years in a Shia-run prison will be hell on a kid like Ismail. Perhaps he'll see his mother again. If he survives, he'll be able to go back to school. He's got a difficult future ahead of him, but at least he'll have a chance.

Nineteen

THE RETURN TO THE OTHER SIDE OF THE HOUSE

YUSUFIYAH, LATE APRIL 2006

THE HELICOPTERS ALIGHT. Barely have their skids hit dirt when the Special Forces leap from their side-mounted benches. They maneuver for the target: a small apartment building sitting in the center of a field of goats. In the moonlight, they dodge the animals and reach the side of the building. The apartment they want is on the second floor.

Stairwells can be death traps in close-quarters combat. The team scales the stairs swiftly and flows out onto the second floor. In the darkness they find the door they want. Now they've come to the most dangerous moment: breaching. The men are at their most vulnerable upon first entry. They don't know what is waiting for them. A booby trap? An IED that will bring the entire building down upon them? Jihadists armed with AKs and a resolve to die in place? Or, as has happened before, will they find an innocent family cowering before their onslaught? Whatever they find, they will have mere milliseconds to decide whether to pull their triggers. The wrong decision will get people killed—both soldiers and civilians.

They breach the door. The first team pours inside. They find an average Iraqi living room, but this one has three sleeping mats thrown on the floor. Motion in the back of the room. A man in a vest materializes from the gloom. Two more shapes move behind him.

The man in the vest detonates himself. The explosion rocks the building. Suddenly, two more blasts follow, one on top of the other. There were three suicide bombers. The first one caused the other two vests to blow. The inside of the living room is sprayed with human mist. The walls and ceiling are streaked with gore. Somehow, none of the soldiers suffers wounds.

They move forward swiftly. In the mess they find a woman, barely alive. Nearby, her unarmed husband lies dead. The woman will be treated, but first the rest of the apartment must be cleared. The team stacks up on a doorway leading off the hallway. At a signal, they storm into the room, weapons ready. Nothing. Another team clears a bathroom. One room left.

Inside it, they find a surprise.

Twenty

TERRORIST FOLLIES

A VIDEO PLAYS ON the flat-screen TV in the conference room. Randy has put the CD in the desktop computer. We saw parts of this video a few days ago when Zarqawi released it as his latest public bid for jihad against our forces. It shows him flanked by masked men with M4s, one of which has a grenade launcher. Later, he blasts through probably two hundred rounds with an M249 SAW light machine gun, insinuating that his men had captured the weapon from American soldiers they'd killed.

This version of the video is slightly different: At one point, Zarqawi is seated between his men spouting hate. But then the camera view changes. He's outside, fumbling with the SAW. He fires a few rounds and it stops. He's puzzled. A hooded terrorist steps from off camera left and charges the weapon by pulling back its bolt. When that happens, the conference room erupts in laughter.

Zarqawi obviously knows nothing about guns. The video

continues; now he's got the SAW rocking. He empties the two-hundred-round box magazine as his minions scream *Allah akbar! Allah akbar!* Everyone's dressed in terrorist black, complete with hoods that reveal only their eyes and the bridges of their noses. Zarqawi wears a black do-rag and shiny white New Balance sneakers that make him look vaguely like a wannabe hip-hop artist. Strapped to his chest is an Eastern Bloc ammo vest—meant for holding AK-47 magazines. The whole scene is ridiculous.

It gets better moments later. Zarqawi walks toward a white pickup truck. In the background, one of his minions carries the SAW by a metal handle mounted on the top of the weapon's receiver. Another minion walks up to the first one. They trade weapons. Minion number two grabs the SAW by the barrel. Big mistake.

Everyone in the conference room breaks out laughing again.

Firing a SAW causes the barrel to heat up, just as it would any other machine gun. Minion number 2 registers heat, then pain, and drops the barrel. Minion number one catches the SAW before it hits the ground.

The video ends a few seconds later.

This is not only amusing, it's significant. This is the raw, unedited footage shot for Zarqawi's latest propaganda video. At the very least we can release this to the media and make him look like a fool. More important, this cut is obviously not something Al Qaida wanted passed around. Whoever this came from has to be close to Zarqawi's inner circle. Randy speaks.

"This video was found on a laptop hidden in the living room of the safe house Abu Gamal gave us. We raided it last night. Inside, the strike team encountered three suicide bombers. All three blew themselves up. None of our guys were hurt." He pauses for effect. I know he wishes he could be out there with them. That used to be his life, and he misses it.

"There were two other individuals in the house. One male. One female. The male died in the explosions. The female died while being transported to an area hospital."

He lets that sink in. "We're close, people. The people inside the apartment obviously knew Zarqawi. One of them could have been videotaping Zarqawi's last release. Chances are good that Zarqawi was at that location in the past few days."

The news electrifies the room.

"There's one other thing," Roger interrupts. This is rare. Usually our interrogation unit commander is content to let Randy run things. This is actually a good thing as Roger's not anywhere near as dynamic or aggressive a leader as Randy.

"In the back bedroom, the team discovered two boys. One is fourteen. The other is twelve. Their parents lived in the apartment and died in the blast. The three suicide bombers were staying with them, sleeping on the living room floor."

They saw the carnage that became of their apartment? Their parents dead on the floor? The suicide bombers blown to bits all over the walls and ceiling? These poor kids.

"Look," Roger says, trying to sound stern. He doesn't quite pull it off. He's too nice. "Nobody talks to these children without my approval, got it? Everything goes through me on this one."

He says a few last words and then leaves the conference room. Randy steps back up in front of everyone and says, "Close the door in back, please." Somebody does. As soon as it is shut, Randy looks around the room. In a cold, stern voice he tells us, "Ignore that. I'm ████████ in charge here. I make the decisions. Got it?"

No argument there.

The meeting breaks up. I head to the 'gator pit to meet with Steve and Cliff. Both Steve and I are qualified to talk with children. As criminal investigators we had to take classes on this issue, and we have experience interviewing them. We have a female 'gator on the night shift with similar qualifications.

I resolve to take the kids. This needs to be handled gently, and they're obviously scared and suffering from what just happened to their family.

Cliff tells us, "Forget about the oldest kid, Jamal. He's mentally disabled or something. It looks like his family pretty much ignored him."

"What do you mean?" I ask.

"Well, they left him out of everything. Apparently, he just stayed out in the fields all day and tended the family goats."

"Okay, what about the younger boy?"

"Naji is his name. He's twelve. And he's a piece of work.

"Last night he told Megan that because she was wearing pants and no head scarf she was an infidel whore." Megan is a 'gator who works the night shift.

"No way," Steve and I start cracking up.

"More than once, actually. He's pretty convinced that all American women are whores."

"Steve," I say, "we're going to handle this very carefully. We won't interrogate, we'll interview. Got it?"

"Of course."

"We won't run any approaches. We'll just ask questions."

"Right."

"You talk to him first."

I walk over to Randy's desk and tell him what we have in mind. He approves. We take up stations. I head for the Hollywood room. Steve retrieves Naji from a storage room where both brothers are sleeping on mattresses brought in for them.

A moment later, Steve and Naji walk into a booth. I put on headphones and tune in.

Steve puts Naji in a big, comfortable, leather chair. The high back and wide arms simply swallow the poor kid. He's skinny with brown skin, a black head of hair, and soft brown eyes that stare intently at whatever he's focused on.

Biggie is the 'terp for this one. Biggie is an Iowan now, but he was born in southern Iraq. He's a huge man with oversized feet, hands, and ears. He's jowly too, with close-cropped salt-and-pepper hair and piercing black eyes. The first time I saw him, he scared the hell out of me, but he's a gentle giant.

Steve starts with basic pleasantries. Biggie translates everything with a soft voice that sets Naji at ease. The boy is matter-of-fact in all his replies. He seems like a good enough kid.

During a lull in the conversation, I see him take the initiative. He rattles off a few sentences, all in that matter-of-fact tone. Whatever he said, it struck Biggie as odd. He looks at Naji, then Steve, then back at Naji. The 'terp shares another exchange with the boy, then sighs.

"He says, 'You Americans are all infidels and deserve to die.' "

Steve looks over at this child. He looks so frail and unassuming. Yet his eyes are lively. What is in them? I can't tell from the monitor.

"Don't you think we're just all people, and we need to get along?" Steve asks. Biggie translates. The boy shakes his head violently. Words pour from his mouth.

"No," Biggie says, "You're all infidel pigs. I can't wait until I'm old enough to cut your heads off."

Such violent words from such a scrawny kid seem so incongruous that it's hard not to smile. Steve and Biggie actually laugh a little. Then clearly it strikes them. This kid has been marinated in Al Qaida propaganda. He's the face of our future. They stop smiling.

Naji shrugs his shoulders. "I hate you all. Someday, I will have my own knife. I will use it to behead infidels."

"He's twelve," I say to myself as I watch spellbound from the Hollywood room.

Steve decides to press on. "Naji, who were the men living with you in your apartment?"

Biggie looks unsure about asking this, but he does it. Naji waves a hand casually, "They are suicide bombers. They came to us four days ago. I know one of them is Saudi, but I don't know where the others are from."

He's using the present tense. Does he not realize they're all dead?

"Do you know who this is?" Steve asks as he shows him a photo of Zarqawi.

"Of course, that is Abu Musab al Zarqawi. He is our hero."

"Your hero?"

"Of course! When we play, the tallest, biggest kid gets to be Zarqawi."

Steve can't help himself. "What do you play, Naji?"

"*Mujahideen.* I will grow tall someday, and then I will get to be Zarqawi." Again, he uses the same matter-of-fact monotone. It gives me chills.

"Why were suicide bombers at your house?"

"They were preparing for a mission. A glorious one."

"What was that?" Steve asks.

"I do not know. Somewhere in Baghdad." Naji pauses, then he falls out of that peculiar monotone. For just a flash, fear and worry creep into his voice. "Where are my parents? Why am I not with them?"

Oh ███ He doesn't know. Go easy, Steve.

Steve looks momentarily stricken. But he rallies quickly and replies, "Your parents are in the hospital. They were injured when the suicide bombers exploded in your apartment."

"Oh. Can I have something to drink?" The monotone returns.

Biggie hands him a Coke. He drinks lustily from the can.

Steve begins to probe for details. Naji is proud to be able to provide them. He tells Steve that his father handpicked him to be a leader in Al Qaida someday. Jamal was the castaway son the father never showed favor toward. Naji was the family's rising star. His dad groomed him well.

"My father took me to every meeting!" he brags.

"Where were these meetings?" Steve asks.

Naji has a remarkable memory. Meeting by meeting, he details who was there, how many guns were stored at the house, what was discussed, and what plans were made. He tells all to Steve without understanding the consequences to his father's cell. From the information he provides, it isn't hard to tell that Naji's dad was a mid- to high-level Al Qaida officer who had ties all over Yusufiyah and the Anbar Province.

By the time the interview ends an hour later, Steve's filled up pages in his notebook with detailed information about Naji's father's network.

Back in the 'gator pit, Steve and I marvel at all the intel Naji has provided—the names, the locations; he's pinpointed the better part of Al Qaida's operation around Yusufiyah. It is amazing.

"The kid brags about everything. He's trying to show me how much his father trusted him."

"I know," I reply. "He has no idea what he's just done to all his dad's friends."

Steve nods, then turns serious. "The kid's been brainwashed."

"Totally."

"Matthew, he's a Kool-Aid-drinking Al Qaida member. At twelve."

"You know the irony?" I say. "He's the only one I've seen here so far."

I marvel at this.

"Me too."

"And he's twelve. Twelve."

"The wave of the future." Steve and I just stare at each other, unable to speak. I know the same thought crosses both of our minds. *How are we ever going to win this war? We can't reeducate all the Najis out there.*

Steve looks out across the 'gator pit. "We're going to be in Iraq a long, long time."

Twenty-one

THE MEDIA MAN

LATER THAT AFTERNOON, I struggle to get through all the reports that have been kicked back to me for various formatting errors. Aside from Naji's wealth of information, we haven't had much progress today. Mary interrogated Abu Haydar. From the Hollywood room, I watched him toy with her again. She and Tom are set to interrogate Abu Bayda later today. I doubt much will come of that. None of the other interrogations are related to the Group of Five except for Steve's session with Abu Raja.

I can't get over Naji. How can a kid be filled with so much hate? How can he be so intelligent yet so totally naïve about the consequences of what he's telling us? No matter. His information will save many lives. Based on his first interrogation. ███████████████████████████████ ██████████████████████ Perhaps we'll get lucky and find another big fish somewhere in the mix.

"Matthew, I hear Steve call to me.

I turn around. Steve looks elated. "What's up?" I ask.

"██████████Abu Raja. You'll never believe who he is."

"What? Who?"

"I told him that Ismail copped to working for him."

"Yeah? What did he do?"

"At first he was pretty shocked. He tried to cover for Ismail. Said he only worked for him one time."

"You know, that's actually pretty noble of him."

"Yeah, I was thinking that too. Still, he admits that he's Al Qaida's media guy."

"What? You mean for Baghdad?"

Steve shakes his head. His grin grows even wider, "For Iraq. For all of Iraq."

"Yeah, ██████████ All those videos—the beheadings, the executions, the attacks on our convoys—all those things came from Abu Raja and his group."

All over Baghdad, anyone can buy cheap DVDs and CDs showing these things. It's Al Qaida's propaganda effort. And they've been kicking our tails for the past two years on this front. Our paltry press releases and leaflet campaigns have not dampened their ability to recruit.

"Great job."

"Thanks. I gotta write it up." He dashes off to his desk and starts hammering on his keyboard.

"I knew it!" I hear Randy exclaim from across the 'gator pit. I see Randy buried in piles of paper. He's examining a photograph and swearing under his breath. He calls Cliff over. "Does that look like Abu Bayda?"

"Yeah, about twenty years ago."

Abu Bayda's the oldest member of the Group of Five.

He's also a source of growing friction between Randy, Tom, Lenny, and Mary. They've been interrogating him without success now for two weeks. For the past few days, the 'gators have been recommending his transfer to Abu Ghraib. Randy's not ready to give up. He's got a feeling about these guys, especially Abu Bayda.

So he's been digging through old intelligence reports. He's been around longer than almost everyone else in the compound. He's the institutional memory here and he's not afraid to go digging through the old files in search of clues. It looks like he just found one.

Abu Bayda's been using a false identity. He's actually Hassan from Tal Afar, and he is the known leader of Al Qaida's operations in northern Iraq. Cliff goes back to his desk and runs his real name through a database.

"Says here his son was just picked up by Iraqi police. He's in a Shia prison right now."

"You're kidding me?" Randy asks.

"No. He's down in Basra. Kid's only seventeen. Look, we have a photo of him."

A flurry of activity erupts in the 'gator pit. Cliff calls down to the prison and confirms they have Abu Bayda's son. The Shia-dominated police grabbed him though he doesn't seem to have done anything wrong. Abu Bayda's real identity is well known around Iraq, especially amongst the Shias he has victimized so thoroughly with suicide attacks and bombings. It seems as if the Shia might have snatched his son as a hostage.

It takes some negotiating, but Randy manages to get him transferred to us. Within hours of his discovery, Randy's got Abu Bayda's son flying to our compound.

Now we have leverage.

I hurry over to the Hollywood room.

Mary and Tom sit down in one of the booths. Abu Bayda comes in, black mask over his face. The guard escorts him to his seat and leaves.

Tom holds up a copy of the photo we've just found of his son, who is in his prison uniform, looking miserable.

"Take your mask off please," Tom tells him.

Abu Bayda does as instructed. The first thing he sees is the photo of his son.

"Your son is in a prison in Basra," Tom tells him.

Abu Bayda can't even respond. He starts to quiver from his head to his hands. His eyes are rooted on the photograph.

"Hassan al Tal Afar!" Tom exclaims, "Your son is in a Shia prison."

"P–p–please," Abu Bayda whispers. He reaches for the photo. Tom lets him stroke his son's face. In past interrogations, Abu Bayda was a strapping and rugged older man in his mid-sixties. He retained an aura of power that Lenny, Tom, and Mary had been unable to penetrate. Now he is deflated. He starts to cry. He throws his hands in the air next to his head and utters Allah's name.

Tom offers him the most addictive thing in the world: hope.

"Hassan al Tal Afar. I can have your son here today. You can see him."

Through his tears, Abu Bayda searches Tom's face. Is this a trick? He's suspicious. Little does he know that his son's already on his way to us.

"My son is not involved," he moans.

"No. He's not. We know that."

"Why is he in a Shia prison?"

"We don't know why, but I can get your son here today."

Tom leans forward and places the photo in Abu Bayda's hands. The old man's fingers are shaking so hard that he nearly drops it. He fixates on the image of his seventeen-year-old boy in a prison jumpsuit. The son of one of Al Qaida's most fearsome leaders, the commander of all of northern Iraq, the boy would not survive in a Shia-run prison. Abu Bayda knows it.

"You can see him. We can get him out."

"How can I trust you?"

Tom leans forward. He says reassuringly, "You help us, and your son will be here."

"You bring my son here. You get him out of that Shia prison forever, and I will tell you whatever you need to know."

"Can we trust each other?" Tom asks warily.

"He is my youngest son. I have tried to shield him from my work. He is not involved in any way so this would not happen." He can't continue. Through more sobs, I hear him struggle to say, "I will help you any way that I can."

"Let's talk then," Tom says.

"No," Abu Bayda regains a fragment of composure. "I won't say a word until I see my son."

An hour later, his son arrives by helicopter. He's immediately brought to us, and a guard brings him into the interrogation booth. His son is so shocked that all he can say is, "Father? Father?" Abu Bayda puts his hand to the boy's head and pulls his forehead to his own. With his right hand he pats his heart. Both father and son weep.

"Alhamdullilah," Abu Bayda says, giving praise to Allah.

I can't help but think that Abu Bayda knows Al Qaida would never be this merciful to one of us, were the roles reversed. He must know what a gift he's just been given.

All too soon, the moment ends. The guard takes Abu Bayda's son away from him and places him in our cellblock.

Abu Bayda collapses into his chair. He wipes the tears away and then looks Tom right in the eyes. Man to man, he says, "Thank you." He turns to look at Mary. "Thank you. Thanks be to Allah. You have been merciful to me."

I hear the words in my head from the meeting a couple weeks ago when I suggested using the Love of Family approach. *When he joined Al Qaida he wrote off his family.* I hear the analyst's laughter.

Abu Bayda takes a deep breath, exhales, and begins to talk.

Abu Bayda swore allegiance to Abu Musab al Zarqawi and Al Qaida. He tells us that he was willing to give his life for him and for the cause. He believes in the Al Qaida ideology. He wants to see a caliphate established and a global jihad unleashed to spread the word of Allah. He also tells us that he is a member of Al Qaida's Mujahideen Shura Council. This is the group of senior leaders who control the war effort against America in Iraq.

Abu Bayda admits to being the leader of the entire network around Mosul and details his logistical operations. Weapons flow in from Iran and are spread through the region. A circuit of safe houses is used to move suicide bombers, weapons, ammunition, and explosives from one area to another. Over the course of the day's interview, he gives us several hard targets.

But he doesn't give us Zarqawi. He doesn't give us anyone over him. And he doesn't tell us why he was in a farmhouse near Abu Ghraib, hundreds of miles from his area of operations. Most puzzling of all, he refuses to tell us any more about Abu Haydar. Why is he protecting him?

At the 2300 meeting we have a lot to discuss. It turns out that we've got two senior Al Qaida officials in the prison. And with the intel we've just gained from them and from Naji, we have enough targets to keep the special forces busy for weeks.

"This is great work, people," Randy tells us. "But we're still not any closer to Zarqawi. We've moved laterally and down, and we're going to be rolling up a lot of networks in the next few days, but we've got to move up."

He slaps Abu Haydar's face on the overhead projector. "Mary?"

Mary stands. "He gave us nothing today. He still maintains that he was only a cameraman."

Randy grits his teeth. "Recommendation?"

"Transfer to Abu Ghraib."

Randy looks at Cliff. Cliff shrugs his shoulders.

"Denied," Randy says slowly. He exhales hard. "We've got to break him."

He looks over his audience. We're all weary. All frustrated. Everyone's been giving all they have to this mission. We score victories, but they are tactical ones. We need a strategic blow, one that will help stop the suicide bombings—one that will stop the civil war. But that one blow seems more elusive than ever.

We're always one step behind Abu Musab al Zarqawi. Somehow, we've got to make up the distance.

Twenty-two

A VISIT FROM THE BOSS

GENERAL GEORGE W. CASEY sits quietly in the conference room for almost an hour as Randy summarizes the past few weeks. The breaks we've made have done serious damage to the networks around Baghdad. As a result, the number of suicide bombings in the second half of April have plummeted. Since the Baratha Mosque attack on April 7, where three suicide bombers killed at least seventy people, there have been no catastrophic attacks.

We're making a difference, even if we haven't made the final jump to Zarqawi yet.

At the end of the briefing General Casey says, "I have a question. Why do they join?"

Randy's ready for the question. He gives the general the standard line. They want to establish a caliphate. They want a fundamentalist state and Sharia law. They want to use Mesopotamia as a base to attack the United States and Israel.

That's not exactly right. I have the chance to influence the senior commander in Iraq and I want to say something.

I stand up. General Casey turns and looks at me. "Sir, that is true for some of the Al Qaida loyalists, but there is a distinction. Since coming here, I've seen many average Sunni who have joined Al Qaida out of economic need and out of fear."

The general gives me an inquisitive look.

"Fear of the Shia militias, the Badr Corps, the Mahdi Army. After we invaded and disbanded the army, the Shia threw most of the Sunni out of work. Then they started moving into their neighborhoods, kidnapping and killing people. Many of our detainees joined Al Qaida simply to survive. They aren't ideologues, and they don't believe in Al Qaida's dogma, but they see Al Qaida as the only entity willing to help them."

I want to say: if we could only harness that, figure out a way to work with the Sunni so that they feel that we are protecting them, that we are their allies, most would turn against Al Qaida.

General Casey's response to me is a dismissive, "Hmm." I decide to keep my mouth shut. Randy's already looking at me with bulging eyes.

So much for that. The meeting breaks up, and I head into the routine for the day. In a few days, I'll lose Steve to an assignment at another station. I'll cover down on Abu Raja and Naji, so by week's end I'll have my hands full. Meanwhile, Tom and Mary are busily working with Abu Bayda. Soon his son will leave for Abu Ghraib to be outprocessed, as will he. Abu Bayda will almost certainly hang. A senior Al Qaida leader cannot hope for much mercy in front of the court, no matter how much information he provides. That said, perhaps his cooperation will buy him some leniency.

His son will be released. He has committed no crime other than being his father's boy. His mother lives in Baghdad, and he will soon be able to return to her.

Naji and his older brother Jamal are still living in the storage room. We bring them extra treats and cups of hot cocoa whenever we get the chance. Meanwhile, we're trying to track down their nearest relatives.

Twenty-three

A SLIP

ABU RAJA STARES at me in complete surprise. His hands clutch the mask he's just pulled off.

"Hello, I'm Matthew. Steve had to leave for a few days, so I'll be talking with you."

"Oh. Yes. Nice to meet you." He regains his composure, but life in the cellblock has not been kind to this pediatrician. I thought he hit bottom last week, but he's plunged even further. He's aged since he's been here, and his eyes betray hopelessness.

"I appreciate your willingness to cooperate with us."

He sighs and recites, "Whatever I can do to help, Mister Matthew."

"I've read the reports, so I know what you and Steve have discussed, but I did want to ask you a few questions."

"Certainly."

"Where did you say you grew up?"

"Mansur. My family is from Mansur," he says bleakly.

"Has it been hard for you to work since the invasion?"

"Yes. After I lost my government job, it has been very hard."

"It is a noble thing, what you do—taking care of sick children."

I see the shreds of his pride well up above the despair for just a brief moment. "Thank you. It was my life's work . . . once."

He sounds wistful. Yearning. That gives me an idea.

"Abu Raja, if you could go back and do things over again, what would you do differently?"

He doesn't even have to think about it. In fact, he looks as though he's thought of only that since he got locked up.

"A few years ago, I received a job offer to work in Qatar. I turned it down . . ." His voice trails off. He fights his emotions. I wait.

"I . . . should have taken it. I should have moved my mother and myself to Qatar. We never would have come to this if I'd just taken that path."

"Maybe you can still get to Qatar," I say.

That barely registers on him.

"I can't make promises, but I've seen others get out of Iraq. We have the power to do that. But it's not easy to convince our boss."

He looks even more miserable.

"What more can I tell you? I've admitted my role. I've admitted who I am. I've told you that I was at the farm-house."

"I know. And I've talked with Ismail, too."

Suddenly, some fight surges into Abu Raja.

"No. Ismail is a confused boy. I only met him one time. He has had very little to do with my operation."

He's protecting Ismail again. Amid the wreckage his life's become, he is trying to do the honorable thing.

"I understand. You know though, there is one thing that still troubles me."

He sits quietly and waits for me to continue. I pause. He continues to wait. I can see him scrape together some defensive energy.

"The thing is, I don't get why Abu Haydar went to the farmhouse with you, Abu Gamal, and Abu Bayda."

"What is your question?" he says that so quietly that I barely pick it up.

"Well, Abu Haydar was released four months ago from Abu Ghraib. Why would he risk going to the house with you after such a narrow escape?"

"I don't know," comes his rote reply.

"Why would he risk capture again?" I am genuinely puzzled by this. It doesn't make sense to me.

"Maybe Abu Shafiq told him."

I freeze.

Abu Shafiq is Abu Raja's boss. Why would Abu Shafiq be talking to Abu Haydar if he were just a cameraman?

I try to keep my face a mask, but I think the shock registers. He's looks at me worriedly, realizing he just gave up something very valuable.

I have to pounce on this quickly.

"When did Abu Shafiq tell him?"

"I'm not sure," Abu Raja hesitates.

"But Abu Haydar and Abu Shafiq met together?"

Desperate, his eyes search the room.

"Abu Raja, are you telling me that Abu Haydar and Abu Shafiq met together?"

"Yes. They met one time."

"Why?" I fire each question at him as soon as he finishes each answer, giving him no chance to think.

"I don't know why they met." It is more lament than answer.

"But they met. Without you?"

He doesn't want to answer that one.

"Abu Raja, they met without you?"

"I'm just . . . I don't know. I've tried to tell you so many things I've forgotten what I've told you."

"They met without you?"

"Yes. That I know of." He sounds like he's just made a confession.

"How do you know they met?"

"I saw them on the street together, talking."

"One time?"

"Yes one time."

▆▆▆▆▆▆▆▆▆▆▆ "Let me ask you this. What can I do for you?"

▆▆▆▆
▆▆▆▆▆▆▆▆▆▆▆▆▆▆▆▆
▆▆▆▆▆▆
▆▆▆▆▆▆▆▆▆
▆▆▆▆▆▆▆▆▆▆▆
▆▆▆▆▆▆▆
▆▆▆▆▆▆▆▆▆▆▆▆

He sighs with relief.

"Thank you. Thank you so much."

"We're here to help."

Ten minutes later, I'm back in the 'gator pit, my mind spinning. We've gotten this all wrong from the very beginning, and I need to think it through. I sit down at my desk and pull out the wire diagram that I've made based on what we thought we knew about the Group of Five.

Abu Gamal is the bomb maker. He was at the house to wire the suicide vests before their mission. Abu Raja is Al Qaida's media czar. He says he's the leader of the group. Abu Bayda, the oldest, turns out to be Al Qaida's northern regional commander. Abu Haydar is just the cameraman.

Baloney.

Maybe we have this all wrong. First, why would Abu Bayda be there? If this was just another preface to a series of suicide bombings, why would such senior men be present? Maybe the target was significant. Maybe this was supposed to be on the scale of the Golden Dome or larger.

That might make some sense. But that still doesn't explain why a regional commander is in a house hundreds of miles from his area of operation. Why would he care about an operation destined to hit Baghdad?

And it doesn't explain what Abu Raja just gave me. Abu Haydar is no cameraman. He met alone with Abu Raja's boss, Abu Shafiq. That strongly suggests those two are either equals, or even that Abu Haydar is Abu Shafiq's boss.

Abu Raja isn't the leader of the Group of Five. Abu Haydar is.

And if he's higher in the chain of command than Abu Raja, that puts him right inside Zarqawi's inner circle.

Why risk bringing so many senior leaders to one suicide bombing preshow? What if they weren't at the farmhouse for a suicide strike?

Holy shit. Maybe we really do have this all backwards. Maybe the suicide bombers were there to protect the Group of Five. They were having a meeting, perhaps to discuss Iraqwide strategy, which would explain Abu Bayda's presence. If it was just a regional planning session, there'd be no reason to have Abu Bayda there. I wish we'd been able to interrogate the fifth member of the group. He might have given us something useful. As far as I know, though, he's still in the prison hospital at Abu Ghraib.

If this was a national Al Qaida conference, there would need to be a leader with higher prestige than the senior propaganda officer and a regional commander. That suggests two things: if Abu Haydar's actually higher than Abu Shafiq, then he was there to represent Zarqawi. If not, either Zarqawi's operations officer, Abu Ayyub al Masri, or Zarqawi would have been expected at the meeting. Maybe both.

Abu Haydar is the key.

PART IV

DICE ROLL

GENERAL ALLENBY: *You acted without orders, you know.*

T. E. LAWRENCE: *Shouldn't officers use their initiative at all times?*

GENERAL ALLENBY: *Not really. It's awfully dangerous.*

—*Lawrence of Arabia*, 1962

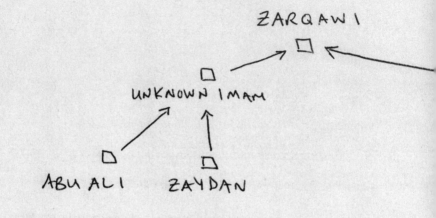

ZARQAWI

UNKNOWN IMAM

ABU ALI   ZAYDAN

RELIGIOUS WING

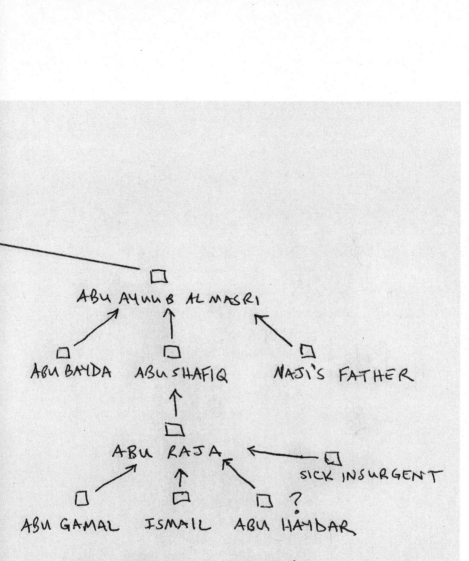

ABU AYUUB AL MASRI

ABU BAYDA   ABU SHAFIQ   NAJI'S FATHER

ABU RAJA   ← SICK INSURGENT

ABU GAMAL   ISMAIL   ABU HAMDAR   ?

OPERATIONAL   WING

Twenty-four

A SINGLE, EMPTY HAND

1100 MEETING, MAY 1, 2006

T HE GROUP OF Five seems to be the compound's only link to Zarqawi. But Abu Bayda isn't talking about those above him, nor is Abu Raja. Abu Haydar isn't talking at all.

Randy's standing in front of all of us. He's put one foot up on a chair again, his signature meeting pose. He's frustrated and angry and filled with a sense of urgency. Not only is the pressure—from the president down to the task force commander—greater than ever, but Randy's a short timer now. He's due to leave us in a matter of weeks and he wants Zarqawi badly. He doesn't want to head home after all this time without accomplishing the mission.

He runs through all our current detainees. We have a new crop. Naji and Jamal are gone. We found an uncle who has taken them in. I can only hope that he'll try to undo the damage the father inflicted on young Naji's mind. That's a thin reed to grasp, though. Chances are that as soon as he can

wield a knife, we'll catch him on one of Al Qaida's beheading videos.

"I know I've said this a million times, but we've got to
pick up the pace," Randy vents. "We've got to close the gap.
Enough said."

He sits down at the head table and calls for the first slide.
Abu Haydar's face appears on the screen in front of us.

At the 2300 meeting last night, Mary had again rec-
ommended his transfer. She still hasn't gotten anything out
of him.

Lenny stands. He looks agitated.

"Nothing to report. Detainee still maintains that he was
only a cameraman."

Randy grinds his teeth. "Recommendation?"

"Transfer to Abu Ghraib."

"Please," I hear Mary whisper from a chair behind me,
pleading.

Randy squints at Lenny. He looks pained and pissed off.
He exhales hard and finally says, "Approved. Get him out of
here."

The meeting breaks up. The last time I asked Randy if we
could put somebody else on Abu Haydar, he made it clear
that would never happen. As I left his office, he told me not
to bring it up again. The look in his eye told me I was dan-
gerously close to stepping over the line.

Abu Bayda is still considered the leader of the Group of
Five. Abu Haydar is still officially the cameraman. Yet everything in me screams that he's the link. He's the guy we need
to get talking.

And it won't happen. Mary and Lenny have tried to control him, but he has maintained control the entire time. He's

played them both and in every interrogation I've watched, it is clear he has no respect for them. In return, they treat him with contempt.

As I leave the conference room, I approach Randy. He eyes me warily, as if he expects me to barrage him with more requests. Instead, I ask, "What time are the prisoners being transferred today?"

"The admin guy says twenty-three hundred hours."

Twelve hours from now. I return to my desk and study my computer monitor.

We're going to lose everything we've worked for with the Group of Five and a shot at Zarqawi. I know it. I can feel it. But, will Abu Haydar ever talk? Our new methods have had success with Abu Ali, Zaydan, Ismail, Abu Gamal, Abu Raja, Abu Bayda, and other small fish. But even they have their limits. Nobody spills all. Except for Naji, that is. Our new methods have rolled up many networks, but Abu Raja, Abu Bayda, and Abu Gamal never gave up their boss.

Maybe our new methods won't work on Abu Haydar either. The trouble is, we haven't been able to try them.

What am I going to do?

Nothing. Nothing can be done. I start editing the day's reports.

I look at the clock. Thirteen hundred already. Abu Haydar gets transferred in ten hours.

I grab a notebook and head over to the Hollywood room. Steve, who just got back to us from his other mission, is in the middle of an interrogation with Abu Raja. Trying to distract myself, I tune in.

It's going nowhere. Steve tries to get him to give up Abu Shafiq, but Abu Raja's not budging. At one point he says,

"I've told you everything I know already. I just want to leave. I don't care about the consequences. I just can't take these endless questions anymore."

I close my eyes and rub my temples.

How many times have we captured so many senior leaders in one place?

Surely, there will be other leads, and other branches to follow. Maybe we can find another way to Abu Shafiq.

I switch to another screen and press a few buttons to listen in. Rachel, a new 'gator, a blonde-haired, twice-divorced mother of three, is going over a map with a former Fedayeen, one of Saddam's personal bodyguards. She's using an approach I taught her that leverages hope. She's mixing new and old methods. In return, the former Fedayeen is providing targets. Maybe there's hope here. I keep watching.

Yet this will take days, maybe weeks, to develop. And in the meantime, how many innocent Iraqis will die? How many American soldiers will be ambushed and killed? How many suicide bombers will turn marketplaces into bloody bedlam?

Abu Haydar is the key to stopping the carnage.

The rules of this game are rigged. Somebody above Randy, above Roger, is micromanaging our unit and deepening the division between the old-school and new-school adherents.

Maybe Abu Raja didn't slip. Maybe he handed me that piece of intel as an approach. He's already proven he can be deceptive. Maybe Abu Haydar is just a cameraman.

No. If he were just a cameraman, he never would have taken the risk of going to the farmhouse—not with one stay at Abu Ghraib in his past. He's committed. He's cunning and highly intelligent. He has all the hallmark behaviors of a leader.

He's the one. I know it. I go back to editing reports.

I look at my watch. Fifteen thirty. An hour and a half has passed. We lose Abu Haydar in eight hours, thirty minutes.

I run to the chow hall to grab food for my new 'gator, who won't have time to make it before the evening meal finishes. I bring the food back and leave it on her desk. I walk back to the Hollywood room to check on the interrogations. Steve comes in and asks for permission to give a detainee an extra blanket. I approve. He says the guy is a nobody, but he's helped a little bit. Maybe that will turn up something. I return to the 'gator pit.

I sit down at my desk and start correcting more reports. The little clock in the corner of my screen reads 1630. I can't stop looking at it.

We're six hours and thirty minutes away from letting our biggest fish slip from our grasp. I read another report.

Across from me, Randy is feverishly sorting through piles of paper on his desk. Occasionally, he utters a curse under his breath. I check the time. Fifteen minutes before 1700. He's scrambling to get his notes together for his daily briefing of the task force's senior leadership.

Inspiration strikes. Perhaps I can use his distraction to my advantage.

No. I've got to play by the rules others have put in place. They're there for a reason, and my role is not to judge them. My role is to uphold them. To respect them.

How many lives will be on your hands if you don't at least try? The window will close in five minutes.

My heart starts to race. I am a major in the United States

Air Force. I take orders. I give orders. I follow the rules. I perform my duty.

I swore an oath to the Constitution to protect this country from all enemies.

Where do we draw the line? If everyone decided they knew what was best for the country, best for their unit and command, no matter what the rules may be, we'd have total chaos. The system would break down.

But this is wrong. We've had the wrong 'gators on the right man for three weeks without any result. Our hands are tied. We cannot try anything new. We can't run another approach. And Zarqawi will slip through our grasp once again. We'll be back to where we were in 2004.

Randy puts a few final pages on top of one pile and scoops them under his arm, looking frazzled.

It's now or never. If I'm wrong, my career ends. I'll be thrown out of Iraq, sent home in disgrace. But if I'm right, lives will be saved.

If I don't do this, will I look back in twenty years and see every suicide attack from now until Zarqawi is stopped as my burden?

An image flickers into my mind from a video Ismail admitted editing. No doubt Abu Raja distributed it far and wide as an example of Al Qaida's daring resistance.

It starts with a typical Baghdad street scene. Men in dishdashas move along, conducting business and buying goods. Women in black burkas hustle past the cameraman. He walks forward through the crowd, and it becomes clear he's following another man dressed in a white dishdasha and a tan linen vest.

They walk past an outdoor restaurant. People sit clustered

around tables, laughing and drinking tea. Parents shepherd children along. One little girl holds her father's hand as he crosses the street from camera left to camera right.

The man in the linen vest continues on. We never see his face, just the back of his head. For a moment, the cameraman loses him in the crowd, but then he spots him again as he emerges near a busy intersection. The camera halts. It zooms in on Linen Vest, who steps between cars stuck in a traffic jam.

The explosion is so intense that the camera swings towards the ground. All we see is pavement, but we hear the sounds of mass panic clearly: screams of agony, pleas for help, sobbing women. In the distance, alarms wail.

The cameraman seems to regain his footing. The scene pans slowly upward. The street is desolate. Bodies lay in heaps. Smoke coils over burnt and blackened cars parked by the curb. A huge charred crater mars the middle of the intersection. A truck burns nearby.

The little girl, at most ten years old, lies in the middle of the street at camera right. Her body is sprawled next to her dead father's. Her hand is stuck straight up in the air, as if her dying act was to reach out for the comfort of her father's grip, only to find empty air.

Our enemy holds this up to the world as proof of their resolve against us.

I will not hate the enemy, but I will do everything I can to stop it.

I stand up. Randy is heading out the door. I give chase.

As I cross paths with Randy in the hallway, I can see that he's agitated and consumed by his thoughts. I mumble as I pass, "Mind if I give Abu Haydar a shot?"

He doesn't look at me. He can't hear me. I'm an aggravation he doesn't have time for right now.

"Whatever," he says.

He strides ahead down the hallway, leaving me in his wake.

I take that as approval and head for the cellblock.

Twenty-five

SIX HOURS

R EMOVE YOUR MASK, please."

Abu Haydar pulls the black mask off his face. He regards me quizzically. I'm a break in the routine—he's never seen me before. Aside from the guards, the only people he's seen for twenty days are Lenny and Mary.

I practiced my tone and opening lines while waiting for him to arrive in the booth, but I didn't have time to think any farther ahead.

"Hello," I say with measured cordiality, "I am Dr. Matthew."

"Hello, Dr. Matthew. I am pleased to meet you." His lips are tightly drawn. He sets his jaw. I can tell by his eyes that he's already sizing me up. The game is on.

"No," I say, letting a little excitement creep into my voice, "the pleasure is all mine. I've wanted to talk to you for a long time."

His eyes widen a little.

"Oh really?"

I need to build rapport.

"I've read quite a bit about you," I say, "I feel like I already know you."

His eyes crawl across my face, studying everything, missing nothing.

"The truth is that I am fascinated by your education in Islam."

Nobody's discussed religion with him. At the schoolhouse, our instructors drilled into us that a discussion like this should be avoided at all costs. They said that to counter some of the attempts at denigrating Islam that took place at Gitmo. Religion has become a taboo subject.

But I've never felt that way. If we can't discuss religion with the enemy, then where are we? Everything starts with dialogue.

"I'm sorry, what did you say?" Abu Haydar replies, his words tightly wound. He speaks English with an upper-class British accent.

I know he's heard me. I'm not sitting knee-to-knee with him, but I am close. I spoke clearly. My comment threw him off his game just a bit.

"How long have you studied Islam?" I ask.

He stares at me, expressionless. Neither of us blink. His eyes are black, almost opaque. I cannot glean anything from them. I can see he's searching my eyes for clues as well.

"I have studied Islam for fourteen years." He lingers over each word, ensuring its perfect pronunciation.

"I have studied Islam myself, but not for the same length of time as you," I marvel.

I stroke his ego and wait to see how he responds.

"You have studied Islam?" he sounds respectful, but there's an undercurrent of disbelief in his tone.

"Yes, I have."

He doesn't react. Instead, he studies me again. He folds his hands into his lap.

I have a card to play here. I pick up my copy of the Koran from the desk and I hold it out to him. He looks at it, and I see his poker face slip a little. He is surprised.

"Is this yours?" he asks.

"Yes. Before I came to Iraq, I was stationed in Saudi Arabia. A friend of mine, a colonel in the Saudi Air Force, gave this Koran to me as a gift."

He opens it, and a card falls out. He retrieves it from the concrete floor and looks it over.

"I've highlighted verses and copied them down. Ones that have themes that intrigue me or that I don't quite understand yet."

"This is the Wahhabi version."

"Yes, it is. The colonel is a friend to this day."

He looks over the Koran. "Is he? Did you like living there?"

I nod and smile, "Oh yes. I loved the hospitality the Saudis are so famous for. I loved to sit and talk with my Saudi friends . . ."

I'm about to go on, but he cuts me off, "What did you talk about with your Saudi friends?"

He's trying to gain the initiative over me. Who is interrogating who here?

I'll go with it for now. Let him get more comfortable. Give up control for something else in return.

"Politics, mainly."

"Oh, so you are interested in politics?"

"I have a doctorate in international relations and culture. It is my passion."

One hand comes up to his close-cropped beard. He strokes his chin slowly, seemingly lost in thought.

"I have a passion for politics, too." He says that as if he's revealing something. Actually, I think he's baiting me.

"Well, we have something in common."

I can't tell what he thinks of that answer.

He shifts gears but retains the initiative, "Have you studied Iraqi history?"

"Yes, I have, actually."

More beard-stroking. Several seconds pass. I wait, letting him keep the initiative for now.

"What is your favorite period of Iraqi history?"

"The twelfth century," I answer honestly. "I am particularly fascinated by Salahadin and his campaigns during the Crusades."

If my instructors at the schoolhouse could see me now, they'd ▓▓▓ bricks. The Crusades?

But he's intrigued. We discuss the Crusades and Salahadin's campaign in Egypt, where through force of personality he was able to rally a Shia-dominated army against a Christian invasion.

Time passes. I try not to get anxious. I don't know how long we've been at it, but it has to be at least an hour.

Abu Haydar smiles and remarks, "There is no doubt that Salahadin was a wise, intelligent leader."

"And merciful," I add.

"That is true."

I decide to grab the initiative.

"Muhammad, peace be upon Him, says it is good to have mercy on your enemies. I believe that."

That got his attention. "Yes. That is part of leadership. It is a balance between mercy and strength."

Was that a signal to me? Before I can respond, he adds, "It is good to show mercy."

That was a signal.

I am about to regain the initiative and ask him a question, but he beats me to the punch. "Excuse me please," he says with almost sterile politeness, "I am sorry. Are you Muslim?"

"No, I'm not. I am a Christian, but I've had an interest in Islam for many years."

The doppelgänger is taking form.

"How did you develop that interest?"

I tell him a true story.

"Back when I was in college, I was always studying religion. I wandered into a bookstore. On one aisle, I saw a copy of the Koran. I picked it up and was looking at it when a black Muslim-American approached me and asked me if I had read the words of Allah. I had not, so I bought the copy of the Koran and read it. I later studied Muhummad, peace be upon Him, and the history of Islam."

"That is very interesting . . ."

"Problem is, I don't think I am strong enough to be a Muslim."

He stops stroking his beard momentarily.

"What do you mean by that?"

"Well, to be a true Muslim, you must surrender to Allah's will, correct?"

"That is correct."

"I don't think I could live up to that."

He laughs at that. "Well, no one is perfect."

I laugh as well. "Yes, we all make mistakes."

His eyes narrow at that reference. His gaze goes straight to my eyes again. He watches with renewed intensity. "Yes, we all make mistakes. But mercy demands forgiveness, right?"

"Exactly."

Does he want to cut a deal? This smells like bait to me. I pretend not to notice and change the subject.

"What sort of sports do you like?"

I see a hint of disappointment and surprise on his face and decide that he liked the direction we were going and make a mental note to revisit it when the time is ripe.

"I like ultimate fighting and mixed martial arts."

"I enjoy both as well."

"Do you practice martial arts?" he asks.

"Yes, I studied tae kwon do for many years."

It's a lie.

He returns to stroking his chin, "I have practiced martial arts for twenty years."

I nod and look impressed. "Martial arts are a thinking man's sport."

Will he notice that I'm stroking his ego?

"That is right." He looks pleased.

"Do you know jujitsu?" I ask.

"No. I have a black belt in karate."

I'm alone, sitting in front of an insurgent who has practiced hand-to-hand combat for twenty years.

There's a knock on the door. "Excuse me," I say coolly as I stand to crack it open. The truth is, my heart jumps into my throat. Have I just been caught? At the very least Randy will be furious with me. He'll probably see that I'm sent home.

I grasp the doorknob and turn until I hear the latch disengage.

I pull back just enough so I can peer into the hallway. Steve's standing there, a Coke in hand. Relief floods through me.

I slide into the hallway. As I do, Steve sees who is in the booth with me. His mouth opens and his eyes go wide. He gives me a *what the hell are you doing* look.

"What do you need?" I ask.

"I'd like to offer some incentives to Abu Raja next time we talk. I need your approval."

"Sure, no problem."

He jerks his head slightly and eyeballs the door at the same time. I shake my head. *You don't want to know.*

"Hey, what time is it?" I ask, just as he's ready to head back to the 'gator pit.

He glances at his watch. "Twenty hundred hours."

I only have three more hours.

Twenty-six

THE DUEL

I STEP BACK INTO the booth and sit down. Abu Haydar has been patiently waiting, his hands folded in his lap.

I pick up right where we left off, as if we have all the time in the world. "I am amazed at your study of martial arts. It must take discipline to devote twenty years to it."

"It requires more passion than discipline," he says in a passionless voice. He's making sure I can't get a read on him from his vocal inflections.

"What sort of ultimate fighting do you watch?"

"I watch the PRIDE Fighting Championships—in Japan. And UFC in the United States."

"I've been a fan of the Ultimate Fighting Championship for several years."

He nods once, then says, "I have watched since 1993."

He one-ups me in everything.

"That was back in the day. They allowed everything back then, didn't they?"

"Yes."

We continue for another hour, talking about our favorite fighters, including the legendary Royce Gracie. It turns out he is a favorite UFC fighter for both of us. Nevertheless, Abu Haydar upstages me at every turn, demonstrating superior knowledge of the sport. Every time I mention a fact or tell the story of a fight, he digs out something more arcane that only a die-hard fan would know.

I don't have to create a doppelgänger; we have many things in common.

The conversation wanders to travel. He's been to Jordan, but nowhere else. When he asks me if I've traveled much, I tell him truthfully, "Yes. I've been to about fifty countries—South America, Asia, Europe, and Africa."

"Which is your favorite country?" I suspect he figures I'll say Iraq to stroke his ego some more. Instead, I surprise him with my answer, "I loved Costa Rica. I hiked in the mountains there, and they're beautiful."

We're running out of time, I have to start something soon.

"I understand you have a family—a wife and three children right?"

"Yes, I do," he says with his typical flat expression. A wave of the hand, and he dismisses this line of conversation. "Tell me, what is it about Royce Gracie you like?"

A quick Love of Family approach isn't going to work here. That's obvious. I decide to roll with it. "I admire his intelligence. He defeats his opponents with his brain."

"Yes, that is true. I also respect him for that. How do you think he will fare in his next bout?"

Gracie's set to fight Matt Hughes at the end of the month.

"I expect he will do well. Matt Hughes has a mixed record. He's the underdog, the up-and-comer, but Gracie's a legend."

"I agree. I think Gracie will win."

I'm running out of patience. We have less than two hours before he is transferred.

I've got a good read on him now after four hours in the booth with him. He has an unusual personality type, one that I've only heard about at our special investigations academy but have never encountered in the real world. He's a grand egoist, absorbed in a delusion of grandeur.

I wonder how I can exploit this.

I change the subject again, wresting control of the conversation away from him.

"I know now that you have studied Islam for fourteen years. What else have you studied?"

A long pause. I sense we're on the verge of something, and he's internally conflicted. His calculating, cautious side urges silence. The grand egoist in him prevails.

"I have studied logic, the art of persuasion, and argument diversion."

No wonder he ate Mary's lunch and rode Lenny in circles.

"Interesting. By the way," I try to change the subject again, "Did you serve in the military?"

He measures his words like a cook measuring flour.

"Well, Iraq fought a lengthy war with Iran. Many Iraqis served in the miltiary."

"Ah!" I interject. "I see you just used your argument diversion skills on me so you didn't have to answer the question."

He laughs gamely and even blushes a little. "Yes, you caught me."

Now, the doppelgänger takes form again.

"I studied logic and persuasion while getting my doctoral."

He looks impressed. He gets my unstated point.

"I was never in the military."

This is the first time he's reacted submissively. He has respect for me. What is my next move? Outside the booth, I hear footsteps in the hallway. Are the other 'gators winding down before the end of the shift and the 2300 meeting? I don't know how much time is left.

He interrupts my train of thought and seizes the initiative again.

"You know, Dr. Matthew, you are not like the others."

He's running an approach on me. I react with caution.

"What do you mean?"

He strokes his beard again and says nothing. He's sizing up my response. Finally, he says, "You understand Muslim history."

"Thank you. I like history."

"No. No. No," his expressionless mask slips away again. Now he looks agitated.

"You know more than those others. They are ignorant."

The schoolhouse taught us never to damage the credibility of another interrogator to a detainee. You never know when that 'gator might have to sit down with your detainee again.

I decide to avoid his gambit entirely.

"Abu Haydar, I have a question for you."

The poker face returns. "Certainly." Again with the precisely pronounced words. He's ever so careful about everything. Where was he going with that approach? Maybe I can find out my own way.

"I've always wondered something about Islam," I say.

"Please, go ahead with your question."

"Do you Islamic scholars ever discuss the word of Allah as passed to Muhammad, praise be upon Him? The thing is, His followers wrote the Koran. Is it possible they made mistakes in the translation?"

He leans back in his chair and steeples his hands. He looks very pleased.

"Dr. Matthew, this is such a good question. I used to work in the Ministry of Religion, did you know that?"

"Yes."

"I was in charge of the Arabic language programs."

"Yes."

"But the study of Islam has always been my overriding passion."

"I wondered if you had thought about this question before," I say, eyes wide with respect.

"It is possible that some of the followers of the Prophet Muhammad, praise be upon Him, made mistakes when they wrote the Koran. But those mistakes would have been Allah's will, so they are still the words of Allah."

"Allah is all-knowing."

"Precisely!" he explains, with one index finger pointed upward for emphasis.

After a short pause, he continues, "Dr. Matthew, I am really enjoying this conversation."

"Thank you. I have enjoyed it, too."

"I have never been comfortable with the others."

He's running that approach again. I want to cut it off.

"I have another question for you."

"By all means, what is it?"

My brain is racing. The clock is ticking. I need to pull together everything I've learned here in Iraq. It's time to warm up the dice.

"In 2003, the United States takes out Saddam. But after Saddam falls, we make many serious errors."

He looks interested. He's stroking his beard again, studying me.

"We disband the army, we hand the government over to the Shia. We let the Shia militias run free and intertwine themselves with the police and the New Iraqi Army—we've made a lot of mistakes."

He nods his head. His eyes are fastened on mine. He's hanging on every word, wondering where I'm going.

"What I don't get is this. Can't the Sunni see what's happening here? Can't the Sunni see the war that is coming?"

"War that is coming?" he asks.

"Yes. Look at what we've done since 9/11. We invaded Afghanistan. We get bases in Central Asia. We invaded Iraq. Turkey is our ally and we have bases there as well. We've surrounded Iran."

"Iran," he says and stops stroking his beard.

"Can't the Sunni see that we've positioned ourselves around Iran? That the real war will soon be with the Iranians? This is just me talking here, but can't the Sunni see this coming?"

He starts stroking his beard again. His studies me intently, looking for any sign, any clue that will tell him my ulterior motive. I give him nothing.

"Yes," he says slowly, "we have discussed this."

"In such a war, the Shia of Iraq would not be on our side."

He agrees. "They most likely would not."

"That's why I'm here."

His hand freezes in mid–beard stroke. He grows absolutely still. Everything in the room, even time, seems to stop.

He stares at me. I stare back.

His eyes no longer study me. They are fixed on mine. He doesn't blink.

He opens his mouth slightly and says in a low voice, "I was wondering why you had come to visit with me."

"I'm going to be straight with you because we don't have much time."

It is an honest admission. Outside in the hallway, I can hear more footsteps heading back to the 'gator pit. The last thing we do before the meeting is send somebody around to empty the trash cans. There's a metal one in the hallway right outside the booth's door. It makes a racket when it's emptied, and it has always annoyed me. It will be my alarm clock now.

He lets me continue. I blow on the dice.

"You've probably guessed that you are scheduled to be transferred to Abu Ghraib tonight."

"Mmm." His response is completely neutral.

"I'm in a position to negotiate with you."

He says nothing. He's scanning my face for any tell, any clue that I am lying.

"I'm on a special mission."

He strokes his beard more slowly now.

"So, what is this mission?"

"I have been tasked with finding Sunni leaders willing to fight with us against the Shia and Iran. We must rebuild our relationship with Sunnis if we are to win this coming war."

He weighs my words.

"Go on."

I'm shaking the dice.

"We need strong, capable leaders whom we can trust and work with closely as equal allies. I think you are one. But before I can offer this to you, I have got to be able to trust you."

He stops stroking his beard again. He remains as still as a corpse. The silence is unnerving. I hear the garbage can clang in the hallway. I'm out of time. This is it. I let the dice fly across the table.

"Abu Haydar, excuse me for speaking so directly. You're supposed to leave in just a few minutes, and I cannot negotiate with you at Abu Ghraib. That would be too dangerous for you. I need to know right now if you are willing to negotiate with me."

The garbage can clangs once more, filling the silence. More footsteps.

His eyes are locked on mine again.

I refuse to speak first.

"You are different. But are you sure you can help me?" he asks.

"I can pick up the phone and call Washington at any time. I can make this happen. But right now, right here, I have to know I can trust you. So, here is what I need for me to trust you. I am thinking of a name. You know who I am thinking of. I know you know. But I need to hear you say his name. Then I know I can trust you."

I have no name in mind. I made it up.

We sit in silence. Every second is agony. I force myself to keep my face a mask. I'm filled with confidence and I feel I can do no wrong. I know I've run a good approach. But there's no telling if he'll take it. The odds are he won't.

Thirty seconds pass. The footsteps in the hallway recede. Everyone's in the conference room. The meeting is about to start.

The silence endures. He scrutinizes me, but I don't move. Every muscle, every nerve must sell this long shot. One twitch, and he'll run away.

A minute has passed. I swear he hasn't blinked.

Suddenly, he opens his mouth.

"Abu . . . Ayyub . . . al . . . Masri."

I'm speechless. Al Masri is Zarqawi's number two man. He just told me he knows Al Qaida's operations officer for all of Iraq. He's no mere cameraman.

I smile warmly. I've got to keep selling this. "Thank you my friend. That is the name. Now I know I can trust you."

██████████████████████████

"How do you know al Masri?"

"We have met four times."

"Where?"

"Farmhouses in Yusufiyah. Al Masri never meets at the same place twice."

I want to continue this, but I don't have that luxury.

"Abu Haydar, I need to leave now for a meeting. I also

need to make some phone calls on your behalf and I absolutely must stop your transfer to Abu Ghraib."

He looks thoroughly relieved, "Yes. Yes. Please do that." This is the first indication I've seen in any of his interrogations that he hasn't wanted to go there.

I get up to leave. "Wait, Dr. Matthew, one more thing. I only want to talk with you."

That's not going to fly. There's no way I can function as senior interrogator and focus' on Abu Haydar. Besides, there's no way Randy will officially agree to have me in here.

"I'll see what I can do. But you may have to talk to some of the others again. Not everyone works for me."

He looks puzzled and disappointed with my reply. Still, I have given him hope, and hope is the most powerful weapon.

He rises and extends his hand. I am taken off guard. Iraqis don't shake hands. I take his hand in mine. He clasps my wrist with his other hand. "Thank you Dr. Matthew. Thank you."

It is a handshake worthy of two newfound allies.

Twenty-seven

A CHANCE FOR UNITY

MAY 1, 2006, 2300 HOURS

EY, YOU'VE GOT to take Abu Haydar off the transfer list," I say to the guard standing in front of a row of prisoners, all of whom are prepped and ready to depart.

The guard replies, "He's supposed to get on the chopper now."

"I know. But trust me, he's not leaving."

Stopping a prisoner transfer requires a small mountain of administrative paperwork and many procedural hoops. My request short-circuits all of that. The guard doesn't look happy. "Fine. But it's on you."

I give him a big smile and a thumbs up. "Yes. It is on me."

I race to the conference room. There is a vacant spot up front where the senior interrogator is supposed to sit. Directly behind that chair is Lenny. I slip into the chair trying to stifle my grin.

I am borderline euphoric. We've got a shot now. If we can properly exploit Abu Haydar, he can at the very least give us al Masri. Al Masri can give us Zarqawi. We're one step removed from a breakthrough. We won't have to start from scratch.

Randy storms into the meeting. He looks anxious. Apparently the meeting with the task force senior leadership didn't go well.

He kicks off the meeting with a few administrative announcements and then gets down to business.

"Slides," he calls.

Abu Bayda's mug shot appears on the flat-screen. Tom stands and describes everything Abu Bayda gave up earlier today. He's still talking about how his network operates and how they get resupplied from Iran. He has not given us anything that will lead us closer to Zarqawi.

Randy thanks Tom. He calls for the next slide. It's Abu Haydar.

"He's on the chopper to Abu Ghraib," Randy says. "Next."

Before the admin guy can click the mouse, I interrupt.

"Uh, the detainee provided valuable information today."

Randy freezes. I hear Lenny intake a sharp breath behind me. There's not a sniffle from Cliff, nor a cough or a sneeze or a shuffled foot under a table.

As if in slow motion, Randy's head turns until his eyes find mine. His head twitches to one side. That isn't a nervous tick. That's his *I'm about to tear you a new cornhole* twitch. He obviously didn't hear my request at 1700. But it doesn't matter now. The truth shall set me free.

"The detainee admitted that he met with Abu Ayyub al

259

Masri four times in different safe houses around Yusufiyah. Recommend we retain and exploit."

Randy's jaw unwinds so far that I'm certain I see his tonsils. He's too stunned to even talk. The room remains silent. It feels like Randy and I are alone even though forty analysts and interrogators are arrayed behind me.

"Wha . . . ho . . . who . . . ? "

I wait. Finally he says softly, "We've never had anyone admit to meeting al Masri."

I can't help but grin. The new techniques have just scored a tremendous coup. This could be a unifying moment for our group. No more cliques. No more administrative headaches and secret meetings. We could finally work together from the same sheet of music.

Randy still looks stunned. "Why is he talking now?"

His eyes say *Why is he talking to you*.

"Maybe because I showed him respect. Then I told him I was the boss here and I could get him a deal."

I hear Lenny behind me exhale explosively. He's not a happy camper. Tough ██ He had a month to do his job.

Randy doesn't acknowledge what I've just said. Instead, he realizes what's about to happen. He flushes crimson and shouts, ██ He's leaving right now!"

"No," I say calmly. "He's not. I already took care of that."

Randy doesn't even ask Cliff for a recommendation.

"He stays. We'll talk more after the meeting."

Randy suddenly becomes all business again.

"Next. Abu Raja."

Steve stands to summarize his day. The meeting continues in subdued silence.

When it ends, Randy looks at me from across the table.

He looks strange. Is it embarrassment? I can't tell. "Good ██████ job." He doesn't wait for a reply; he just gets up and walks out the door.

Behind me, an argument breaks out. Lenny yells at Cliff, "No way! I'm not interrogating him any more!"

He sees me watching and turns his fury on me. "You! You just completely undermined a month's worth of work! You just blew every piece of control I had over him. Control is Interrogation 101!"

I wonder if he's about to come after me. I stay calm, but I'm still blunt. "Lenny, how much control do you think you had over him if he was about to be transferred?"

██████████████████ he roars, and as he storms off he adds,

In the back of the conference room, Nathan's still in his chair with a deer-in-the-headlights look. "That was ugly," he manages, as he watches Lenny leave.

I shrug. It doesn't matter. The path to Zarqawi leads through Abu Haydar. We're still in the game.

Twenty-eight

TREASON

AFTER THE FIRST solid night of sleep I've had since getting to Iraq, I roll into the 'gator pit about an hour early. I want to go over last night's reports and see who ended up interrogating Abu Haydar. As I come in, I see Randy already at his workspace.

"Good morning."

He grunts at me, then returns to a pile of paper he's wading through. Nothing can dim this mood, so I press on cheerily, "Randy, given what happened yesterday, is there any chance we can put Tom in with Mary on Abu Haydar today?"

He nods, "Yeah. I'll make it happen. I'll want you to give them a full brief. Tell them what you did and give them some ideas."

"I'd be happy to do that."

I walk across the 'gator pit and sit down. The latest reports await. My mood spirals downward when I see that Lenny interrogated Abu Haydar last night.

I start reading his summary.

"Interrogator had to spend entire session explaining to detainee that previous interrogator is not the boss and had no authority to make any deals. After that, interrogator spent two hours reasserting control over detainee."

I want to scream. I can't believe what I'm reading. Lenny undermined everything I did yesterday. And for what? Jealousy? He's compromised the best lead we've had to Zarqawi in the three years we've pursued him.

Fury wells in me.

The night shift's senior interrogator sits nearby. I print the report and go over to him. I grit my teeth and try my best to be polite. "Did you see Lenny's report?"

The night shift senior interrogator shrugs. "Take it up with Roger. I want nothing to do with this."

I walk down the hall and knock on the door. He's got somebody inside. I don't care. I step inside and say, "Roger, we have to talk. This can't wait."

The other visitor leaves.

I've got to get Roger to act, but I've never seen him discipline anyone. One of our 'gators a few weeks back told a guard to roughen up a detainee at an outstation. The local commander called me and told me what happened. I talked to the 'gator, confirmed the story, and told him to pack his bags. Nobody who pulls a stunt like that with a detainee can ever be trusted inside the booth again, and the task force has a clear zero-tolerance policy for such things. Roger called him back to our prison and let him continue interrogating. He never disciplined him.

I'm not hopeful.

"We have a serious problem." This gets his attention.

"What?"

"Lenny has endangered our best lead to Zarqawi."

I explain the situation. Roger doesn't seem to get it. When I finish, he's not angry—he's not even upset. He asks me to sit down, which I decline, and then says, "Look, we don't want to do anything that could damage careers, okay?"

"Roger, this is not about careers. This is about the mission. You *cannot* let this go."

"I'm sure Lenny has a perfectly good . . ."

"He has sabotaged an ongoing operation. This is treason. We can't trust him to interrogate."

He thinks about this. "Tell you what I'll do for you, Matthew, I'll bring Lenny in here and ask him to delete those sentences from his report. Okay? Problem solved."

"What the hell are you talking about? We have the most important detainee in Iraq in our cell block. He is a direct link to Zarqawi, and Lenny deliberately destroyed our chance to get further information out of him!"

"Powerful words. Let's just take care of this with a few deletions."

I can't win. "At the very least, you've got to pull him off Abu Haydar."

"No, we can't do that."

I'm in a looney bin. Did my commanding officer just tell me the 'gator who failed for almost a month and then pulled this stunt is going to remain in the mix? I can't believe what I'm hearing.

I leave in disgust.

Back at my desk, my mind pours over the damage. How can I fix this? What advantages do I hold here?

One, Abu Haydar doesn't respect Lenny. That's important. That may limit the damage he was able to do.

Two, we have established a measure of respect. I have shown respect for his religion and culture. I will have to hope that works in my favor.

Culture. Maybe there's something I can use there to repair the damage.

Maybe not. Abu Haydar was already paranoid and ultra-suspicious. I can't see fixing this now.

Wait a minute. Paranoia. Suspicion.

Iraqis are total conspiracy theorists. They've been marinated in so many tribal plots and counterplots over the decades that these things come naturally to them. What's more, they love being a part of a successful conspiracy. All someone needs to do is come up with a believable one. One that offers hope.

Twenty-nine

THE SECRET DEAL

A FEW WEEKS BACK I saw a car bombing on film. It was another one recorded for Abu Raja's network and edited by Ismail. It showed a building two stories tall with a pair of humvees out in front. The camera, which the insurgents positioned on a rooftop nearby, captured a squad of American soldiers as they rushed inside the building.

It was a clear setup. The scene shifted, thanks to a neat little edit of Ismail's. Now the camera showed a teenage boy, eyes wide and glazed, sitting in a truck. Somebody handcuffed him to the wheel. He didn't even seem to notice. I wondered if he was drugged up.

The cameraman walked to the back of the truck. Here, a group of insurgents finished arming a bomb. They placed it in the truck bed. The driver's door closed. The truck engine revved, and the scene shifted back to the rooftop. There, the camera followed the truck as it roared toward the humvees, gaining speed block after block.

I wanted to scream. I wanted to turn away. I couldn't do either. I remained rooted in place, watching Ismail's work.

The explosion knocked the entire building down. The humvees disappeared amid the rubble, smoke, and dust.

I hope Lenny doesn't have a conscience, because the rest of his life he will have to live with what he did in a moment of weakness and spite.

I've learned my lesson. Whatever I do in the booth with Abu Haydar has to remain between us. I trust my enemy more than my colleague.

At my desk, a plan develops in my mind. I take no notes. I just spin it and test it again and again in my brain. It could work. But if anyone finds out, I'll be on the next flight home. I'm skirting some rules, operating in gray areas, but if this works, we'll be back in the game.

Nobody has said at this point that I cannot interrogate Abu Haydar. I go and check him out from the cellblock, then wait for him in the booth. As I sit there, I rehearse my opening lines. He's got to buy this right away. If I have to work him, he's lost. He won't talk.

A guard escorts Abu Haydar into the booth. He sits down, and I ask him to remove his mask.

He looks relieved to see me. Thank God.

"Abu Haydar, how are you?"

"I am well, thank you Dr. Matthew."

Do I detect just a hint of distrust? I guess that's to be expected. I know this man. I know how he thinks now. If I am very careful, I can outmaneuver him and turn all of the day's negatives into positives.

"Are you ready to continue?" I ask.

"Yes, I am, but I have a question first."

"Anything, my friend. What is on your mind?"

"Do you really have the authority to negotiate with me?"

I lean back and say, "Ahh. Is that what is bothering you?"

"Yes."

"Abu Haydar, I'm going to tell you something, and I think you'll get the picture."

"Go ahead."

I stand up and pull my chair next to his so that we are sitting almost side by side, facing opposite directions. Our faces are a foot apart, and I lower my voice to almost a whisper.

"Not everyone here works for the same people. Do you understand what I'm saying?"

The subtext here is simple. ███████████████

███████████████████████████████████

███████████████████████████

I'll give him just a little more. "Some of those who work for a different agency from mine have different motives, my friend."

He looks cautious, but at the same time, very intrigued. "What are those different motives, Dr. Matthew?"

"I will be blunt with you, Abu Haydar. Not everyone wants to work with Sunnis."

"Do you?"

"Yes. That is why my boss in Washington sent me here."

"I see." His voice goes vanilla again. He's studying me with those unbelievably perceptive eyes.

I decide to continue.

"I have a certain authority here that others do not. I have the ability to work with Sunnis. Other people resent that. Now, do you still want to work with me?"

Another pregnant pause. I'm naturally impatient, so this is starting to drive me crazy. But I don't speak. My face remains cordial and earnest.

He strokes his beard. He nods once. "Yes. I want to work with you."

"Okay. I want to bring you into our program and get you out of here. I will take care of you. But I need you to do something for me."

His face goes blank. His eyes shine with suspicion. "What?"

"You must never tell anyone here that we have made a deal. It will be our secret and a secret between us and my bosses in Washington."

I've just made him a part of the conspiracy.

He nods his head in a knowing, worldly way. "I understand completely, Dr. Matthew. I will say nothing of our arrangement."

"Good. I must depend on you for that. If you talk to anyone about this, I will have to call off our deal, and Iraq will suffer for it."

"I want to join your program. You have my word."

"Okay. Here is what's going to happen."

Now he leans forward. I lower my voice to an even softer whisper.

"I have to fly back to Washington today to convince my bosses that you are worth the risk. I have a good feeling."

"I understand."

For the next hour, we discuss al Masri. Abu Haydar provides more details of how he operates, and I take notes. He's giving us a gold mine of information. At the end of our session, I tell him, "While I am gone, I need to know you will work with the others here."

His face looks sour. "I would prefer only to talk to you."

"I will be gone. But I will monitor the reports and check on your progress. Don't worry, I will return in a few days, and we'll talk again."

"I look forward to that."

"So do I, my friend. So do I."

Thirty

STASIS

LATER THAT DAY, I sit down with Tom and Mary for a strategy session. I am amazed at the difference. Instead of scoffing at what I've got to say, Mary listens quietly and appears to internalize what I say. "Look, Abu Haydar is a man who needs his ego constantly stroked. Do it in subtle ways, and he will respond."

"How?" Mary asks.

"Small compliments. Make him feel important. Build up respect; don't try to attack him."

"Okay," Tom says.

As for Lenny, I can't get him off Abu Haydar at night. I have no control over the night shift, and Roger's already ruled against me on that. Whenever we pass in the halls, he doesn't even acknowledge me. I do the same. I cannot respect a man who is willing to sell out his mission to settle a personal score.

Over the next four interrogations, Abu Haydar refuses to

give Lenny anything. With Tom and Mary, it is a different story. Little by little, he shares enticing tidbits of information.

But he doesn't move us up the ladder. By day four, little progress has been made. I wish I could do these interrogations myself, but that will never happen. I must work in the background.

I've got to get him moving again. That night, I walk back to the cellblock and ask the guard to let me into Abu Haydar's cell. I find him resting on a mat placed atop a concrete slab that serves as his bed.

The guard steps outside but remains close. I cannot tip my hand to him. Not now.

"Dr. Matthew, how are you doing?"

"I am fine. I have just returned from Washington."

"And what did you learn?" He no longer acts. We are co-conspirators now.

I whisper into his ear, "I've talked with my bosses. Most of them think that you are a good candidate to join the program. So far, though, a decision has not been made."

He looks disappointed.

"How close am I?"

I pretend to consider this. Finally, I tell him, "I would say you are at about forty percent."

He stifles a gasp. Now, he's worried. "Only forty?"

"If you help us, then I think you will get approved."

"Okay. I will." He nods valiantly, but his face is still a picture of concern.

I put a hand on his shoulder, "Abu Haydar, I think this is the beginning of a beautiful friendship."

He smiles back at me, but I can see the *Casablanca* reference is lost on him.

The next day, Mary and Tom sit down with him. I watch from the Hollywood room. Abu Haydar tells them, "I have a friend. He is an imam and he is my friend and mentor."

Tom appears excited. "Who is this friend?"

Abu Haydar ignores the question. "We have been best friends for most of our lives. We have studied Islam together for fourteen years."

Then he drops a bomb, "He knows many things."

Mary and Tom try to get him to define that, but he won't.

After they go in circles for awhile again, Mary asks him, "What is your friend's name."

He will not answer. Instead he tells Tom, "You know, I am very bored in my cell."

"I'm sorry to hear that."

"I wonder if it might be possible to get a book to read."

Tom hedges, "I will look into it. What sort of book would you like?"

"I am very fond of Harry Potter."

From the Hollywood room, I can't help but break out laughing. Imagine if J. K. Rowling knew that one of Iraq's master terrorists was a fan of her work. I later approve this incentive, and Tom finds a copy of a Harry Potter book in the compound. It is delivered to his cell.

The impasse continues for almost two weeks. What has he told us? Is his friend higher or lower on the ladder? Toward the end of the third week, I visit him again in his cell. This time, I find him engrossed in *Harry Potter and the Prisoner of Azkaban*. He's reading it a second time.

We need him to give up al Masri. But he deflects every question with vague answers. "Last I heard, he was in Ramadi," was his last answer as to the whereabouts of Al Qaida's master bomber.

"Hello, my friend," I say as I enter his cell. This is my third visit here. The last time I sat down with him, I told him he was at sixty percent.

"Dr. Matthew, thank you for coming to see me."

"My pleasure. How is the book?"

"Oh, very good. I love Harry Potter. These books are so imaginative."

"I like them too. That one's my favorite," I reply.

He looks ready to discuss the book with me, but I haven't actually read it so I hurry to change the subject, whispering so the guard won't hear. "I want you to know that I have some good news."

"Really? Please share it."

"You're doing great work. I've got everyone on board except the chief of our agency. The others have signed off on you joining our program."

"That is excellent news. How close am I?"

"You're at ninety percent. We just need one more push to bring you to a hundred percent, and then my boss will be convinced that you can be trusted."

He thinks this over. Finally, he whispers into my ear, "Dr. Matthew, later today I will give you something that will change his mind."

"I hope so." He takes my hand and squeezes it in a friendly gesture. As I get up to leave, I tell him, "You know, Abu Haydar, I want to you play a role in the future of Iraq."

"Thank you, Dr. Matthew. Just wait. Just wait."

Thirty-one

THE UNKNOWN IMAM

MAY 15, 2006

"**M**Y FRIEND IS Sheikh Abu 'Abd al Rahman. His mosque is the one in the Mansur neighborhood of Baghdad."

Tom and Mary look on quietly. Abu Haydar's started talking.

"He is Abu Musab al Zarqawi's personal spiritual advisor."

In the Hollywood room, my pen falls out of my hand.

Abu Haydar is not finished, "If you want Zarqawi, watch al Rahman."

He's just given us our first direct lead to Zarqawi.

"What should we watch for?" asks Mary.

"Look for him to drive in a white sedan. If he stops and changes cars, and that car is a blue sedan, he is on his way to see Zarqawi. He will switch cars in the middle of his trip."

In the 'gator pit, Abu Haydar's information ignites a flurry of activity. Randy's already passed it up to the task force commander. We send all available assets to the Mansur Mosque. In the meantime, more assets are mobilized for the chase.

We get our first break when we identify al Rahman leaving the mosque. After that, he goes nowhere without American eyes watching.

At first, nothing happens. Days pass. We wait and watch. On May 31, I walk into the 'gator pit and see everyone clustered around computer monitors and the flat-screen television.

"What's going on?" I ask Steve.

He leans over and whispers, "This is a live feed from a surveillance asset. We're watching al Rahman. He just switched cars to a blue sedan."

This is our moment. I'm captivated by the street scene on the monitors. The blue sedan stair-steps around Baghdad. The asset follows it through all its maneuvers.

The blue sedan makes another sudden turn. It drives behind a tall building and disappears.

"No! NO!" somebody moans.

The camera pans up and down the street. No sign of the car. The asset flies around the building, camera panning this way and that. Nothing. The blue sedan has simply vanished. Along with it went our best shot yet of capturing Zarqawi.

Randy sinks into his desk and utters a curse. He leaves for home in just a few days. Edith, the analyst who doesn't believe Al Qaida operatives maintain their family ties, is scheduled to take over his role. He looks absolutely devastated. He's devoted the better part of three years to this pursuit, and to come this close and miss must be like a knife to the gut.

At least, that's what it feels like to me.

Thirty-two

THE SEVENTH OF JUNE

THE ASSETS PICK UP al Rahman again at his mosque a week later. He can't even go to the bathroom now without being watched. Every house he visits, every location he drives to in his white sedan is noted. If we get another opportunity, nobody in Zarqawi's inner circle will be safe.

This morning Cliff comes running into the 'gator pit. "They've got the blue car again!"

We switch to the live feed from the surveillance asset. The blue car weaves through Baghdad traffic. At one point it stops at a house, but al Rahman does not get out. Our SF teams are on a hair trigger. The moment they get the order and location, the helicopters will be off and racing.

The blue sedan starts moving again. The driver negotiates northeast Baghdad—a heavily Shia area. Then he continues outside the city limits.

"Which way is he going?" somebody asks. We all shrug. It's impossible to tell from the feed.

Cliff stands next to me, "Damn, Matt. I hope we get him this time."

I say nothing. I'm superstitious. I just wish Randy were here, but he's already left.

The car drives down a highway for almost forty minutes. It turns off the road into a small neighborhood and pulls up to a house. A man comes out of the house and switches with the driver, but al Rahman doesn't get out of the car.

"I guess Racer X is driving now," Steve says.

The car pulls out of the driveway and returns to the highway. Finally, it turns onto a minor road and then pulls up to a farmhouse. A few outbuildings are scattered around the property.

Al Rahman opens the passenger door and climbs out of the sedan. He walks inside the house, trailed by his driver.

Somebody shouts, "They're en route!" They needn't have bothered. The helicopters buzz our hangar as they fly overhead toward the most important target of the Iraq War.

This is our moment. We could change history, ending the reign of terror of one of the most prolific mass murderers of our time. I can't even move. None of us can.

The helicopters disappear into the distance. Their beating blades grow faint, then quiet.

I hear somebody ask, "How long 'til they get there?"

"I don't know. That car drove a long way."

The surveillance asset stays focused on the house.

"I wonder if Zarqawi's in the house," Cliff says.

"He's there," I whisper to myself.

Ten minutes pass. No sign of the helicopters. The 'gator

pit's mood changes from expectant to anxious. Are we going to miss him again?

Suddenly, the screen grows dark. There's a collective gasp in the pit. A towering column of smoke and debris erupts over the house. Everyone erupts in spontaneous applause.

My God.

Before the smoke can clear, another explosion tears through the remains of the house.

Cliff runs to make a phone call. The feed ends. We all look around at each other. *Is it over? Did we get him?*

Minutes drag by while we're left in suspense. Finally, an officer walks into the pit.

"Ladies and Gentlemen, we got him. Abu Musab al Zarqawi is dead."

KILLING THE HYDRA

FALL 2006

T HE OCEAN LOOKS sweet today, with perfect rollers that break fifty yards from shore. The sun-burnished beach stretches for miles in each direction. I am home, which for me is on my surfboard and where the waves are.

This is my time. I've lived a nomadic, sometimes fierce existence in the service of my country. I have rarely had a place to call my own, so I return to these shores after every deployment to find solace. My mind clears, and I can make sense of all the things that have happened to me since my last visit.

After my time in Iraq there is much I need to consider. I step into the froth at the edge of the waterline. A few splashes, and I'm waist deep in the balmy ocean. I study the way the waves are breaking. I'm alone on this beach. The weekend families, the bikini-clad women are hours from taking up space on the sand.

Epilogue

I suppose everyone who returns from Iraq must carry their own personal demons. Mine have haunted me since the day Zarqawi died in our air strike.

The strike team reached the house less than a dozen minutes after the bombs reduced it to smoking rubble. As the Special Forces jumped from the helicopters, two Iraqis emerged from the wreckage carrying a stretcher between them. Zarqawi lay on top of it, and when he saw American soldiers approaching, he tried to roll off the stretcher and get away, even as he coughed up blood. A soldier grabbed him and held him in place. As more blood poured from his mouth into the sand around him, his lungs collapsed. He looked up into his enemy's eyes and died.

The strike team brought his corpse to the compound along with al Rahman's. Abu Haydar had pleaded with Mary and Tom to keep al Rahman, his closest friend, safe. He died in the blast, and they later told Abu Haydar. His reaction was the same as Abu Ali's—total emotional collapse.

I saw Zarqawi's body later that day. He lay on the floor at my feet, looking remarkably intact. The bombs had collapsed his lungs, but he had no external injuries save a few cuts.

Not long after that, the entire interrogations unit was called into the conference room for a briefing from a senior colonel and his deputy, a major. They were high-level intelligence officers for the command, but I'd only seen them a couple of times before, during VIP visits. The colonel addressed us with a backhanded compliment, "You all did great work here," he told us, "even though this came down to just a few interrogators." I wasn't sure what he meant or who he meant, until I learned that Mary, Lenny, Tom, and Cliff were subsequently called into the commanding general's office and awarded medals. Lenny, as the only military person, was given a Bronze Star. Finally, a lightbulb went on in my head. I finally knew who tied Randy's hands and why Roger wouldn't discipline Lenny. Most likely this colonel and major called those shots.

The next day, as I walked past Mary in the 'gator pit, she called me over to her desk. "Does this girl look like al Masri?" she asked me.

She held a photo of a dead child—a girl. Her crushed head lay amid the rubble of the house. I looked away, ashamed and horrified. Two children had died in the bombing. Nobody knew who they were.

For me it doesn't matter. I own a part of their deaths and I will carry that guilt for the rest of my life.

The sun is low on the eastern horizon. The water ahead is glittering gold from its reflection. I step into deeper water. The smaller swells bulge across me on their way to the waterline. I slip onto my board and start to paddle.

Killing Zarqawi dealt a blow to Al Qaida in Iraq but it didn't end the suicide bombings. The news still holds tales of horrified shoppers struggling from the wreckage of once-thriving Baghdad marketplaces. We didn't save the day as our leadership hoped we might.

But an organization can only take so much damage. In the wake of Zarqawi's death, we launched sudden strikes all over Baghdad, Yusufiyah, and Anbar Province. Our intelligence brought down dozens of cells and networks. Suicide bombings plummeted for a month. I would like to think that with Zarqawi's death, we helped make Iraq a little safer, even if only for a little while. We brought justice and we saved lives. Over a year later, General Petraeus reached out to

Sunni nationalists and armed them, finally delivering on my promise to Abu Haydar to work together and forget the past, and many Sunnis have in fact turned on Al Qaida. Perhaps an ultimate showdown between Shia and Sunni still looms on the horizon, but with negotiation and understanding, the Iraqi people might someday learn to live together again.

In the meantime, the hydra still lives. Al Masri took over for Zarqawi, and nothing changed in the compound but the target. I left the compound not long afterward to work with a Stryker brigade combat team in the north of Iraq along with Mike, one of the agents I had deployed with. We took part in raids, interrogated detainees at the point of capture, and expanded on the new methods. I carried an M4 and strapped on my Kevlar every night as we left the wire. I felt free out there with the soldiers, far from the politics of our 'gator unit, and I felt that we were making a difference. But it was never as gratifying as that one day in June when I played a role in the death of the most wanted man in Iraq.

I find the sweet spot in the swells. I swing my board around and start paddling hard. The next wave rushes toward me, taking shape in the otherwise amorphous ocean. I watch it over my shoulder, timing my next move. The base takes shape. It starts to curl.

In a heartbeat, I'm on my feet, the board aligned below. Then I'm shooting down the face of the wave as the curl breaks behind me. It is a glorious moment full of translucent sunshine and the perfume of salt water.

The ride ends, and I start paddling for the next wave. I am free again, and one day I will make sense of it all and feel whole.

I think back to those meetings in Abu Haydar's cell.

Those moments crystallized for me the importance of our new techniques. They give us flexibility, insight, and information. Those are the real weapons in the War on Terror. We don't have to become our enemies to defeat them.

I see Abu Haydar again. He leans into me as I speak into his ear, the guard nearby oblivious to our secret deal. And therein lies the most important truth of this new age of warfare. A few words, furtive and whispered, can change the world.

Acknowledgments

M Y DEEPEST THANKS go to John Bruning for his discerning ear, writing, friendship, and dedication. With a surgeon's precision he excised my memories and helped me transform them into a story. My agent, Jim Hornfischer, provided keen advice and took a chance on this book and me, which deserves double recognition. The superb editing and guidance of Hilary Redmon at Free Press was instrumental in excavating and polishing the bones of this story and I am deeply grateful to her. My sincere gratitude also goes to the entire Free Press team for their contributions to this book.

I am indebted to Mark Bowden for his advice on writing, introductory words, and for inspiring me to put pen to paper.

I have no words to describe the feelings of pride that emerge when I consider the men and women that I served with in Iraq. The interrogators who worked for me and the analysts that supported us, many of whom are not mentioned in this book, were, nonetheless, remarkable. The same can be said for our interpreters, the guards that protected us, two Jordanian officers, and our support personnel. Special thanks to my good friends and fellow 'gators, Mark, "Ann, Steve, and Mr B."

I was counseled throughout the writing of this book by several close friends and family members. Each of you offered unique and invaluable opinions for which I am forever thankful.

Today, there are thousands of Iraqi refugees who have helped the American government and whose lives are endangered due to their affiliation with us. The List Project is a U.S. non-profit organization with the belief that the United States Government has a moral obligation to resettle to safety those Iraqis who are imperiled due to their affiliation with the United States of America. To learn how you can help visit TheListProject.org.

Finally, I strongly oppose the use of torture or coercion in interrogations. It is against my fundamental beliefs as an American.

Matthew Alexander

I T HAS BEEN a tremendous honor to work with Matthew to bring this, one of the biggest success stories of the War on Terror, to an American audience. Matthew: Thank you for your friendship and our many off-topic conversations that taught me more than you'll ever know. Our collaboration was one of the highlights of my writing career. Your insight and wisdom, introspection and intelligence have been a source of inspiration and education for me. Writing this book with you opened my mind to so many things, both professional and personal. Thank you for this opportunity. I've grown both as a writer and as a person, thanks to our friendship.

To Jim Hornfischer, my friend and agent, you are the Jerry McGuire of this shark-filled business—honest, humble, talented, and relationship-driven. Thank you for taking a chance on me two years ago, and thank you for everything that you've done for my family. You changed my life, Jim. For that I owe you a debt that I will never be able to repay— but I will keep trying, anyway!

Hilary Redmon stepped into the project early in its gestational phase and provided tremendous guidance. Hilary, it has been a great pleasure to work with you and the rest of the team at Free Press. Your editing has made this book so much stronger and compelling that whatever success it enjoys will be largely thanks to your eye and effort.

No writer can exist in a vacuum, no matter how hard we try at times. In my case, when I begin a collaboration such as this one, I work long hours as the story takes shape. My family, Eddie, Renee, Jennifer—you suffer through these times with such good spirit, support and heart that I cannot help but to love you all a little harder for it. You are the wellspring of all my energy. Larry and Mary Ann, your excitement and encouragement always provides a boost. John Sr., Judy, and Sherry—thank you for your enduring support.

At crunch time, I have many who take care of me here in my little Oregon town. Andy and Denice Scott, you guys are the best. Angie, Becca, Brenda, Alyea—you put up with me and my stacks of paper, books and notes during the busiest times of the morning. Thank you for suffering through my many intrusions into your work day!

Acknowledgments

Bob and Laura Archer—my friends for these past fourteen years—your generosity will never be forgotten.

Mark Farley, whose eyes and insight made no small contribution to this book, is the sounding board every writer dreams of having. He's honest and holds nothing back. Thanks Mark, you helped set us on the right track.

Shawna Akin, who has been my assistant since I wrote *Crimson Sky* back in the late '90's, has suffered my many instances of organizational-impairment with excellent humor and spirit. You keep me on the straight and narrow, Shawna, and I will always appreciate that.

To the 973rd COB's—Bethany, Spencer, Shaun, Joe, Andrew, Joey "The Irreverent Reverend," Aaron, Brad, Taylor, Gaelen, Logan, Ox—and everyone else—your support and enthusiasm helped fuel this project. Your dedication and desire to make a substantive contribution on drill weekends remains a source of supreme inspiration. I'm proud to be associated with all of you, and humbled by your sacrifices and sense of patriotism. Each one of you embodies the best of what it means to be an American.

John Bruning

About the Authors

Matthew Alexander served for fourteen years in the U.S. Air Force. He has personally conducted more than 300 interrogations and supervised more than 1,000. He was awarded the Bronze Star for his achievements in Iraq.

John R. Bruning is the author or coauthor of nine books, including *House to House* by David Bellavia. He has been a military historian, writer, and consultant for eighteen years. He also currently serves as the president of the 973COB.org, a nonprofit corporation that provides training support for the Oregon National Guard, SWAT teams, and local enforcement.